Women In The Wings

20 Biblical Monologues

Jacqueline Sharer Robertson

CSS Publishing Company, Inc., Lima, Ohio

WOMEN IN THE WINGS

For more information about CSS Publishing Company resources, visit our website at
www.csspub.com or e-mail us at custserv@csspub.com or call (800) 241-4056.

Cover design by Barbara Spencer
ISBN 0-7880-2387-X   PRINTED IN U.S.A.

This book is dedicated to the ancient women of faith without whom God's biblical witness would be incomplete.

It is also dedicated to the two congregations who have encouraged these and other creative ways of sharing the gospel: the people of the Wilmot and Mt. Horeb United Methodist churches in Wisconsin.

Acknowledgments

I truly give thanks and praise, for it is the Holy Spirit of God who co-authored this book, providing inspiration and idea after idea. Jesus walked beside me on this journey, often appearing in the faces and voices of these *awesome* companions: my husband, Byron; our children, Alaina, Jasmyne, and Caleb; my parents, Barb and Don; *Computer Guru Extraordinaire*, Chris McCreary; my clergywomen's coaching group; and so many more.

Table Of Contents

Introduction

Welcome to *Women In The Wings*. I share this collection of sermon monologues with you as a local church pastor concerned with communicating biblical truths to people who need their healing, transforming power. I also share hints as a performing artist to help maximize the effect of these truths on those watching and listening. These are sermons first and foremost, bringing to life voices from our biblical past to challenge our spiritual present and encourage choices for a faithful future.

Preaching the Word provides a tremendous opportunity to offer our creative talents and spiritual passion up to the Holy Spirit's crafting. But, if this is the case, why are there days when well-prepared sermons seem to bounce off our congregations like ping pong balls? Perhaps the Parable of the Sower can give us a clue.

In Matthew 13, Jesus describes seeds, the Word of the kingdom NRSV, being planted four times. The seeds and the sower remain consistent, yet the four plantings yield four different results due to one variable: the quality of the soil. As the Apostle Paul pointed out in 1 Corinthians 3, only God can make the seeds grow, though we plant and water. Yet, I believe the Holy Spirit does lend us ways to soften the ground.

Jesus gave preaching concepts life by telling stories that utilized familiar images. Thus, he reached people in the language of their everyday existence. The sermons in this book seek to do the same thing, softening hearts by sharing the soul-searching of human beings much like themselves. Would these dramatic sermons continue to have the same impact week after week? I doubt it. But, every so often, they can aerate the soil, ushering in a breath (*pneuma*) of fresh air.

As I have preached these sermons over the years, a certain phenomenon has arisen again and again. I receive feedback, real feedback, from folks who ordinarily leave church with a simple, "Good to see you, Pastor." Children and teens, visitors, people who attend worship because a family member *makes* them, suddenly share comments about a sermon that they will remember. Even the faithful folk who pay attention week after week express appreciation for the fun and involving proclamation they experienced that day. It seems they needed a new type of sermon to draw in different nutrients to replenish their spirits.

If you are not an actress, do not panic! You are a woman of faith who wrestles with sin and grace just as these women did. Draw upon the part of yourself that you recognize in each of these characters. Memorizing the text is beneficial and allows the character to speak directly to the congregation, yet the story will still speak if you find you need to (subtly) look at a script. I have also included some dramatic tips in the paragraph titled "Making It Play" that accompanies each sermon. Feel free to utilize as few or as many of these ideas as would be appropriate in your setting. Have fun, and so will your congregation.

"Making It Preach" underscores the theological emphasis the sermon states or implies. If you are concerned that the congregation will be more entertained than transformed, feel free to highlight these points in a verbal or printed introduction or conclusion.

Two of these sermons are written in verse to utilize the lyrical rhythm of poetry, to set an atmosphere, and to move the story along. The verse forces an economy of words, while allowing more picturesque images than ordinary speech. It may take a few stanzas for people's ears to adjust, but they will be soon be drawn in as the story progresses.

The most important thing is for you to get to know these real and might-have-been real women as sisters on the great journey. Listen to their questions and allow the answers they discovered to inform and move you. When you let their stories become part of yours, the congregation becomes part of that story, as well. With hearts and senses open, with the ground thus prepared, Christ can indeed grow a harvest that yields a hundredfold. May it be so!

Lectionary Year
A, B, Or C

The Transfiguration Of Our Lord
Matthew 17:1-9; Mark 9:2-9; Luke 9:28-36

Perched On The Edge Of Heaven

Making It Preach

The transfiguration of Jesus was an awesome event filled with theological meaning, but how does it affect the person in the pew? Here is a woman who, like some of them, is struggling with the dissonance between the mystery of God and her rational mind. The transfiguration was confirmation for Peter, James, and John that Jesus was Son of God. Simon Peter's wife grapples with how knowledge of Jesus' true identity should, and actually would, affect her faith and life. With the amount of information provided by science and technology today, there is a tendency to shrink mystery into the category of a problem to which the answer is not yet discovered. Yet, the explosion of interest in our society dealing with spirituality points to new generations that are less afraid of mystery. Therefore, discussion about Christ's divinity and the mystery of the Holy Spirit among us is important in pointing people beyond living a "good life" toward being transformed by the only one who is good.

Making It Play

This interpretation places Simon Peter's wife in her younger adult years, with a young child and reference to her mother's menopause. However, by deleting or changing those comments, her age could easily be adjusted upward with integrity. She could be described as no-nonsense, moving with purpose, competent in the life of a multi-tasking housewife, mother, fisherman's assistant, dutiful daughter, and responsible member of the community. Her discussion with the congregation is an intentional exercise in which she analyzes the unraveling of her carefully woven existence. Her

13

confidence also begins to unravel until she arrives at a plan, only she lays out this plan with caution due to the vulnerable nature of approaching Jesus about something so personal. A simple tunic with or without head covering would be fine, since this takes place in the middle of the night. However, if your hairstyle is short and/ or obviously modern, you may wish to bind or cover it.

Simon Peter's Wife Struggles
With The Implications Of The Transfiguration

I know I'm going to regret this! Pacing the house when I should be sleeping. With so much to do tomorrow, I'll be exhausted halfway through the day! My cousin's family is joining us for the sabbath, and my mother will have her hands full with all of the children, so it is up to me to be cook, hostess, servant, and problemsolver. Simon will be his usual jovial self, but he's useless around the house! Or, maybe I should start calling him *Peter.*

That is the name his renegade rabbi, Jesus, gave him. I say that about Jesus with the greatest affection, though that wasn't always the case — just as I could never bring myself to address Simon by this new name Cephas, Peter in your language. It means "rock," which is a great symbol of strength, but unfortunately I always associated my husband with things less steady, less predictable. Wind, maybe, since he is certainly full of hot air, or fire, burning with passion, but needing to be safely contained — no, my Simon was never the rock. But, then again, that was before....

Frankly, the change in him is why I'm having trouble sleeping. I think I'm getting too old for his mood swings. It's bad enough dealing with Mother's, but at least hers are a natural, predictable part of her getting older. My father, rest his soul, sweet, simple man that he was, would not have known what to do with her! But, Simon, uh ... Peter often has me in a tailspin, whether it is trying to keep up with his exuberant new ideas or fishing him, the fisherman, out of the depths of disappointment. He is rarely anywhere in between, or he wasn't until yesterday. And, his calm steadiness then, more like a rock than I'd ever seen, startled me, and actually makes me a little nervous.

Let me back up. Simon, and he was Simon then, had been going on about a new boat he was looking to purchase, a larger one that would allow him and his father and brothers to take in a greater number of fish with each catch. Of course, somebody, probably a wife or two, would have to sew some of the nets together to make bigger nets until they could afford buy the strongest ones. But, since this plan was more practical than some and might lead to the ability to buy some of things for the house we could really use, I felt myself warming to the idea. And, then, what happened? He came home one day and threw it all out the window! He said he was going to become a disciple of a man who might be the Messiah! Trying to control my temper, I reasoned with him.

"A disciple? Do you mean like Andrew did with that John the Baptizer? You used to complain about how you had to pick up the slack when your little brother wasn't there, and now you want to do that to your other brothers? And, your father is getting older, Simon. He is already slowing down. And, what about us? You don't spend much time at home as it is. Your son is growing and changing every day. He's already itching to go to the shore with you."

"And, I promise I will take him!" he said with that disarming grin, as he caught me up in his arms and, well, hushed my objections in a rather effective way. What could I do? What I have always done, not the least of which was to try and explain it to my mother in such a way that she didn't have a fit. But, she did, especially when she heard about this man who was teaching Simon.

"Nonsense and magic spells, that's all it is! He tells crowds of people that they are blessed if they are poor — ha! — and that they should pray for those heathen Romans who have taken our land and rub our noses in it every time they get the chance. Pray for them! There must be some magic that he uses to make it seem like he is healing people. And, the people he touches — ach — filthy! What kind of a holy man would defile himself in that way?"

Of course, she changed her tune, and so did I, when she fell into a high fever. I thought she was going to join my father in his everlasting rest, and so did she. But, Jesus came into the house, he touched my mother's hand, and the fever was gone, just like that! The next thing I knew she insisted he sit down and that she, not me, serve them all. After that, she wouldn't let anyone say one word against her beloved Lord's Anointed. I still wrestled with wanting Simon to be home more when they left home for longer and longer periods of time. But, I did not want to get in the way of the Lord's work being done by this good teacher, if he thought he could use Simon. The term, *Lord's Anointed*, was a bit strong for Jesus, in my opinion, but there certainly was something about him. People either loved or hated him. That's when I dubbed him the *Renegade Rabbi*, and Jesus just laughed.

As you can imagine, with things being that rough for Jesus, Simon had his tunic all in a knot a great deal of the time. But, this last week was the worst I had seen him. About a week ago, he came home with this triumphant look in his eyes and strutted around the house like a rooster, crowing about how he was the only one of Jesus' disciples who was sure that Jesus was indeed the Messiah. And, because of that, Jesus told him he was Peter, the rock on which his great assembly would be built. My, you should have heard the plans this Peter had for revolution; it was frightening! He sounded like a zealot, ready to expel Pilate and his cohorts by force and set Jesus on the judgment seat, to judge all with justice and mercy. The Herods would have to be dealt with, too, of course, but they'd be like plucked chickens with Rome gone. On and on he went. But, within a day or two his excitement was replaced with heavy brooding, something about Jesus saying he had to die, thus squashing Peter's plans for glorious revolution!

He remained in that funk for the balance of the week, until he came home yesterday this changed man, this ... rock. And, when I asked about the change, he told me more than I wanted to know, more than my practical mind is able to deal with. At first he hesitated because Jesus had sworn him to secrecy. But, seeing the concern in my eyes, he told me that since we had become one flesh and he knew that I would never break his confidence, he would share something wonderful with me. I only tell you because you already know the end of Jesus' story, while I am only now getting glimpses of it.

Peter told me that Jesus took him, along with James and John, up into the mountains, higher than they had ever gone before, until he felt they were perched on the edge of heaven. Then Jesus' appearance began to change, to glow. But, that was only the beginning! Next, Moses and Elijah appeared. I don't know how he knew it was them, but I suppose God was revealing knowledge as this whole thing progressed. And, finally, after Peter made some silly remark about building shelters for the heavenly visitors, a huge cloud descended, and out of it, the voice of the Lord spoke. Peter swears God said something like this, "This is my Son, whom I love; with him I am well pleased. Listen to him!"

"But Peter ..." was all I could get out. My husband looked at me with more gentleness, more love than I had seen in years, probably because I called him by his new name. He held me for a long time, and he felt solid. Then, he fell into a contented sleep, as my mind began to churn. This goes against everything I am sure of, everything on which I base my life. Though I believe in the concept of the Lord Almighty, I roll my eyes when people say they have seen visions. Wishful thinking, that's all it is — or, at least, most of it. I know the beauty and complexity of this world are far too carefully designed to be some kind of cosmic accident. So, obviously the Lord has the power to reveal divine knowledge, but to such fools? And, then they parade themselves about as if they know everything and are somehow better than everyone else!

At least Jesus' teachings, though they seem confusing at first, make sense. God did not create all of life to serve puffed up princes and wealthy merchants! Those of us who have a little more than enough to live on should share it with those who struggle. And, though loving our enemies is difficult, living with war and resentment will be much harder in the long run. If the Lord can show mercy on us with our many mistakes and selfish hearts, we should be able to cut one another a little slack! Yes, there is much that Jesus says and does that encourages my heart and increases my faith. But, this ... this *thing*, this vision, whatever you want to call it, that Peter experienced, disturbs me more than I could ever explain. I think that is because part of me really believes it, or wants to, even though it makes no sense to my rational mind. People glowing, men returned from the world of the dead, God speaking in a cloud ... what does that have to do with my life of raising a

17

child, running a household, entertaining a renegade rabbi and his even more questionable band of disciples? What does it have to do with me?

I'm jealous, I think, that Peter has found this peace and a deeper faith, and I just go through the motions every day of my life, and I never feel different inside. He believes in the miraculous so easily, and I can't — or I won't, something stops me. Maybe it is because I feel like one of us needs to keep her feet firmly planted on the ground. But, maybe not. Maybe I'm just afraid. Yes, me, the steady one, afraid. I'm afraid because this world is changing, and I cannot continue to fix everything and make everything better, not by myself, not when I wake up to a different world every morning! I'm afraid that this new Peter will turn back into Simon and leave me hanging out here all by myself!

I think I may try to talk with Jesus about this. In fact, I think he's been waiting for me to talk with him, and though I've successfully avoided ever sitting still long enough for that to happen, now is the time.

Pray for me, will you? And, pray for the other people like me, who have trouble believing beyond what they see and know for certain. If Jesus really is the Son of the Almighty, then we are the ones who will have the hardest time believing it and accepting the divine gifts he offers. I need to get used to praying, too, I suppose. Whenever I do, I feel like I'm just talking to myself. I know Peter would help me with that, if I'd let him. I guess I need to trust him more. I'd better join him before he comes looking for me. Thank you for your ears and your prayers. The Lord bless and keep you ... in wonder and faith.

The Ascension Of Our Lord
Acts 1:1-11

Gone, But Not Forgotten

Making It Preach

Great mysteries of God, like the ascension of Jesus, make the most sense when viewed through childlike lenses. That is the perspective of the woman in this monologue and may well be the perspective of many new or marginal believers. Grief that Jesus left, true joy that he returned, a need to hold onto the promise that he will come again, and a sense of excitement at receiving his special gift of the Holy Spirit: Does our intellectualized faith have room for such passionate and single-minded emotion? Jesus warned his disciples who were filled with visions of greatness, *Truly I tell you, unless you change and become like children, you will never enter the kingdom of heaven. Whoever becomes humble like this child is the greatest in the kingdom of heaven* (Matthew 18:3-4). This woman exhorts us, "Don't forget him!" But, do we?

Making It Play

This speaker is not necessarily developmentally disabled, but she does look at the world and Jesus with innocence and instinct more than logic and common sense. She could be any age. She would still be in an apron and probably continues to limp a bit due to her fall. You may want to do part of the monologue seated for that reason, unconsciously rubbing the ankle now and then. But, a bum ankle does not dampen her childlike enthusiasm when she speaks of a continuing relationship with Jesus, the cook, and even the congregation. The listeners should feel such warmth and sincerity from her that when she asks that they not forget her, they are ready to smile and say, "We won't!"

A Tagalong Follower Of Jesus
Tries To Understand Why Jesus Ascended

I ran up the hill as fast as I could, my heart was pounding and the sun was hot, but all I could think of was him. I left the pots warming and ran, with the cook yelling after me. I didn't care, even though I knew it would mean a beating when I got back. I had to see him. Word had been filtering through the community that Jesus was alive, that he'd been appearing to certain followers: some of the women, Peter, and others. But, I needed to see him. I had gone and pleaded for my job back after he was crucified. I was scared and had no one; I wasn't anybody important, just a follower in the crowd. So, I stayed here, afraid, yet waiting for any word at all as to what the disciples might do next. Then, just this morning, the brother of one of the disciples made a delivery to my master's kitchen and he told me I might see him if I hurried.

There, up ahead, I could see a crowd around him, listening to something he was telling them, just like before, and then the next thing I knew I was on the ground and my ankle was throbbing. I had tripped over the limb of a fallen tree and had to be careful to pull myself out without getting scratched from head to foot. When I was back on my feet, limping, I remembered what I was looking for and turned back to the crowd. But, it was the strangest thing. They were all completely still and looking up. So, I looked in the same place, and I couldn't move, either! *(points up)* 'Cause, there was Jesus, floating up and away, until a cloud covered him, and that was it. He was gone. I didn't know what to think, and I don't think anybody else did, either, 'cause we all just stood there, looking up, then looking around, then up again. And, I suddenly felt alone, all over again. When I looked back at the group, they were talking with two men I'd never seen before, and they began to cheer. I didn't get it. So, I hobbled over and asked a woman named Joanna what was going on. She said that God just took Jesus to heaven, but the men said that someday he will come back the same way he went. She also said that Jesus told his disciples if we wait here in Jerusalem, he will send the Holy Spirit on us.

"What's that?" I asked.

"It is the power from God," she told me, "that Jesus has been promising. It will turn the disciples into witnesses so they can spread his message, and it will be a comfort for all of us and keep us connected with Jesus."

"Can I have some, too?" I blurted out. "I don't want to lose him, even for a while."

She gave me that kind smile that a lot of people do because I say what I think too fast and have trouble making sense. "We won't lose him anymore," she told me. "Now that he is alive, he will always be with us."

"So, he's coming back from up there?" She shook her head and said someday, but until then, we won't be able to see him. He will be with us, though. I still didn't get it. And, she got caught up with the others who were praising God and hugging each other. I stepped back. I couldn't understand why everybody was so happy. Jesus said that he would be raised again, but I didn't think it meant he'd be raised all the way up there! How can he still be with us if we can't see him and hear what he has to say? And, how long before he comes back?

I just miss him so much, kind of like I do my mama. She died when I was nine years old, and I don't even remember my papa. He was killed by Romans for resisting some order. I lived with relatives in Cana, then in Jamnia, then Bethany, and finally I went out and got this position, 'cause I didn't have a dowry for marriage. But, I heard Jesus when I was visiting back up in Galilee, and he said that all who did the will of God were his brother and sister and mother. I felt my heart get warm because I finally felt like I had family, even if I never got up the courage to talk to him. I followed him, though, everywhere I could. And, he knew me, and he would smile at me whenever he saw me out in the crowd. I always try to do what I think God wants, and until I worked for the Romans, I observed all the laws of Moses. So, I was his sister or mother or brother — well, maybe not his brother! Now, I'm by myself again. I'm pretty used to it, but it sure felt good to think I was important to somebody, important enough to call me sister, even if it was only for a couple of years.

For now, we are supposed to just wait, she told me, for the Holy Spirit, some power Jesus said we will receive. He did say once that if we believe in him, he would put a light yoke on us, not like those big old wooden ones they put on the oxen. Boy, a light one would make my work easier. I usually work twelve or thirteen hours every day, even the sabbath. I don't know, maybe if I pretend I'm working for Jesus, it won't be so bad, especially if I can sort of be like him. I am not very useful. I'm not real smart. But, I am pretty good at being nice to people others forget about, since I'm one of those people. And, if he is really still with us, maybe I could even talk to him, so long as I'm careful others don't see me and think I'm crazy 'cause they don't see him! Maybe I wouldn't feel so shy now that I can't see him.

But, wait! Would that be like praying? Would God get jealous? I don't want that to happen! But, isn't Jesus the Son of God, like the disciples were saying he is? If that's the case, then maybe it wouldn't matter to God whether I spoke to Jesus or to God, 'cause I'd still talk to God, too, and God has got to be awfully busy listening to everybody, anyway. I suppose if you talk to God, and I talk to Jesus, they would give each other the message, right? Oh! And, you know what? If God gives me a message that I think you should hear, I could tell you, and maybe you could tell me if you get a message I should hear! Maybe that Holy Spirit we're all waiting for would help us to know which messages we should keep and which ones we should pass on! This could be fun! You know, if you do the will of God ... you do? ... well, if you do, like Jesus said, then you are his brother or sister or mother, too. Don't you get it? That would make us related!

My ankle hurts! That won't be the only part of me that hurts when I get back to the kitchen and the cook gets her hands on me! I tried to tell her once what Jesus said about forgiving your brother or sister 77 times, but she didn't think that was a good idea. Oh well, maybe I will get through to her, yet. And, even though she hits me when I do something wrong, I pray for her because nobody really likes her, and I know what it's like to be by yourself. I wish she had seen Jesus. I suppose I'm the only one who can explain to her what he's like, even though I really don't want to go back to the kitchen. Maybe when that Holy Spirit comes, the disciples will have something for me to do.

Well ... I'd better get back. I don't really want to leave now that I realize we're family! Oh, well, maybe I'll see you when the Holy Spirit comes. I don't know what that will be like, but if Jesus leaves by flying up through the clouds, I bet he'll send this Holy Spirit in style! Make sure you come out, then, and maybe you can get some of that Holy Spirit, too! And remember, Jesus isn't really gone, 'cause if you know him here *(points to heart)*, that is how close he'll be. Don't forget him, or me, either!

Year A

Who You Callin' A Big Baby?

Making It Preach

This simple, dramatic exchange places a contemporary example of destructive disunity among younger generations (gang warfare) into the early Corinthian church, demonstrating how immature and deadly such conflict can be. This scenario still occurs in too many churches when certain people or ideas are worshiped above Christ, and evil has a field day! Paul spent much time trying to help the diverse populations within early Christianity focus on what unites, rather than what divides them. Today's churches would do well to chant together his words whenever conflict threatens: *There is no longer Jew or Greek, there is no longer slave or free, there is no longer male and female; for all of you are one in Christ Jesus* (Galatians 3:28).

Making It Play

This scene should be played as a confrontation between a woman and her little (late teen or young adult) brother. Or, if a nephew would make more sense in your case, change the appropriate references. His words are assumed. Our speaker is steaming mad and quite comfortably pulls rank over this errant young man on behalf of his sick mother. Part of her frustration comes from her love for him and a desire to protect him and their emerging faith community. His hostile energy is barely contained, but it is no match for his sister/aunt, whom he recognizes as an authority figure and for whom he also feels affection. She should look at him as if he were sitting toward the front of the congregation: close enough for a one-on-one lecture, but far enough away to let the onlookers in on the action. A stola, the female alternative to a toga, simple jewelry, and sandals would be fine.

27

The Corinthian Conflict
Described In Terms Of Gang Warfare

(voice calls from place unseen) Hey! Who you callin' a big baby? That would be you, Disciple Geek!

(running in, pulls invisible young man away from the window) What do you think you're doing? You want them to throw more rotten figs in here? It took us a week to get the smell out last time, and Mom is getting sicker every day. I'm sure she'd really enjoy that lovely aroma hanging over her mat!

(pause for his words that the congregation does not hear)

No — don't even say it! What do you mean it wasn't your fault — how were you tricked? Sit down. I said sit! It is high time you had a talking to, and I don't think Mom is in any shape to do it. Take that off. *(swipes arm band)* What is this arm band? Some kind of a sign that you're in the Jesus Kings? Oh, now I get it. The ones with the ankle bands must be the Apollos Disciples. This is just great! Our brave young men, the future of our faith, are becoming first-century gang bangers!

(pause)

No, you may not get up! You're not going anywhere! Look, I love you. You're my little brother, and I wouldn't let anything happen to you. But, I'm getting scared, here. We're lucky to find any kind of work at all in this town because of being followers of The Way of Christ. We get threatened at the synagogue, looked at funny on the streets; the heat is up high enough without you guys going at each other's throats over whether Paul or Apollos is right about how we should practice our faith. They are not Jesus!

(pause)

Maybe they didn't always agree about what Jesus said, but that's not as important as us sticking together with our eyes focused on the Lord. Is this what you would like Jesus to come back and find? Instead of love for one another, a bunch of arm and ankle bands? What's next? Are you going to start burning out our people's homes, all in the name of Christ? Come on! You know that wasn't Jesus' style, and it shouldn't be ours, either. Didn't you hear that letter from Paul read when we last gathered?

(pause)

Yes, I know you are standing up for Paul and trying to defend him to Apollos' crew, but you don't seem to remember the point of that letter. Paul didn't want us to be arguing with each other. He said that was a sign that we were still a bunch of big babies, spiritually immature. Now, it would be one thing if you were out there defending Christ to those who don't believe in him, but you're not. You're too busy fighting about which of his servants, Paul or Apollos, should be the authority. Why can't they both be?

(pause)

Yeah, you're right; this is Paul's ministry. Paul was first, but in his letter he went out of his way to say that he and Apollos are on the same team. You didn't hear that part of the letter, did you? You were too busy looking at Phoebe and Joanna across the street! *(paces a bit to calm herself down — notices the garden out back)* Look out there. Paul compared us to a garden, like yours. He said that he came to plant the seeds about being saved by Jesus, then Apollos came to water those seeds, giving us additional guidance and encouragement. Wait — let me finish! But, Paul, your great and glorious Paul, said that the growth comes only by God. Paul and Apollos were only doing the jobs God assigned them.

(pauses to take that in)

No, I don't think Apollos is coming back to do any more watering. Chloe just received a letter from Apollos saying that he is no longer planning his follow-up work here precisely because of the division he seems to cause. Apparently, he wasn't aware of how much charisma he's got. And, though I know this is going to get your goat, I can understand why people are so enamored with his preaching. You have to admit that man has been gifted by the Holy Spirit to proclaim the gospel! He speaks with such power that people are drawn to him and his message. He is interesting because he's different. He has those penetrating African eyes and the smooth voice of a trained orator. We don't hear that much around here! When he speaks, you can't help but pay attention, and it is so obvious he loves the Lord. We can feel that love when he teaches. It makes people that much more committed to changing the way they live so that they can be faithful followers of the Christ.

(pause)

Okay, maybe he doesn't do anything for you, maybe he bores you to tears, but that doesn't mean his teaching is bad. He did a lot to help our community grow. And, no matter what you think about his leadership, he is your brother in Christ, like Paul. So are the Apollos Disciples, ankle bands and all.

(pause)

So what if they were the ones throwing those rotten figs? If they did something to you, do you have to retaliate? Have you forgotten Jesus' teaching about turning the other cheek?

(pause)

No, you're right. You are not the Son of God, that's obvious. But, God loves you, anyway, and so do I. Come on. You don't need this arm band, do you? Please, I don't want to see you get hurt! Your little niece and nephews are going to need a loving, righteous uncle who can teach them to put Christ before loyalty to any person or religious ritual. Can I trust you to teach that? Huh? Yeah, I thought so. *(looks at congregation)* Can I trust you to teach that? *(shaking head affirmatively)* Yeah, I thought so! May the Spirit bless your teaching!

Seven Miles Of Miracle

Making It Preach

We are never told the identity of Cleopas' companion, so it could well have been his wife, sister, or daughter. This monologue makes that assumption, as well as placing her in the garden at the time of Jesus' arrest and in the room with Jesus' other disciples when he greets them with "Peace be with you." Jesus' return and explanation of his role as scriptural Messiah brings enlightenment to their minds, but not necessarily forgiveness for their unbelief. This sermon starter explores the naked awareness of sin that comes in the presence of Jesus' truth and how that evokes in his followers the desire to repent and come clean so that a new beginning is possible. No matter how far we wander down the road that leads away from trust in God, Jesus will reveal himself to us and offer us a new path. What we do about that makes all the difference.

Making It Play

A rumpled, dusty tunic, a head cover that could be falling off, and beat-up sandals would give the impression that she has just hurried over seven miles of dusty roads and fields. Yet, the adrenaline of not just the journey, but why she made the journey, keeps her from feeling any weariness — she is actually quite keyed up. She needs to visibly see Jesus enter at a certain place above the heads of the congregation. She needs to hear his remarks in her head so that she may respond believably to him. She hangs her head when she makes her confession, perhaps even falls to the ground if she can do so and remain seen and heard by the congregation. His proclamation of love fills her with release from the guilt, slowly raising her head/body and spirit as she makes her final comments.

From The Road To Emmaus
To The Room Of Skeptical Disciples

Seven miles there we walked, drooping heads and dragging feet.
But, seven miles we've returned, no more burdened with defeat!
"Such a journey!" you may think. "You didn't stay to rest a while?"
How could we sit or sleep: barely a thought, those seven miles?
It is here we need to be. It is you we need to see!

We're speaking puzzles, aren't we? Forgive such great to-do.
But, hearts so full and minds a-spinning sent us straight to you!
No thought was given to the telling, but the telling's why we're
   here.
We saw our Lord! There, we've said it! Let's back up and make it
   clear.
Jesus is alive and well. So, listen close to what we tell.

This morning, all looked gray. No excitement sparked our journey.
We went to visit family, to escape Jerusalem's churning.
To Emmaus we were bound, though we could hardly look ahead.
Thoughts still lingered on the prophet in a borrowed tomb, stone
   dead.
Our talk was all a jumble. Into a stranger, then, we stumbled.

In our apology, he saw our grief, and asked about the cause.
We knew he did not come from here! His question gave us pause.
What else would Jews discuss, whether friend or foe or neither?
The Galilean's trial was far more interesting than the weather!
Such ignorance in this man. I wanted him to understand.

So, I began to tell him of this man from Nazareth,
a prophet, wise in word and deed, who three days past had met his
   death.
Our priests and leaders were the ones who plotted out his downfall,
though we had hoped he'd be the one to redeem proud Israel.
He listened hard, then shook his head. We were startled when he
   suddenly said,

"Fools you are, and slow of heart to believe what the prophets
　　spoke!
When you heard your scriptures read, did you think it all a joke?"
Having gotten our attention, he began, then, to offer
what the law and the prophets said, how the Messiah was to suffer.
So much hidden; now, we know. He showed us how it all was so.

He gave us much to ponder as we wandered down that road.
When we reached our destination, he bid farewell and turned to
　　go.
But, we couldn't let him leave and face the dangers of the dark.
"Stay with us, tonight. Sup and rest before you start."
So, he joined my cousins' family. Astounding things, we soon would
　　see!

The meal was being cleared away when the three of us stepped in.
Then, our feet washed, my cousin brought a loaf for us to begin.
When I moved to break the bread and divide it on our plates,
our guest reached across the table, touched my arm and told me,
　　"Wait.
To your hospitality, I make a toast. Let me, now, become the host."

Our thirst satisfied with wine, the loaf he lifted up.
He gave thanksgiving to our God for the bread on which to sup.
Then, he broke the bread, amazing this, and handed me a piece.
As I took the bread, our fingers touched, and I was filled with
　　peace
that passes understanding. Then, I saw his presence, so commanding.

How we missed it before, we do not know, but we surely saw it
　　then.
This stranger's face became familiar, he looked just as he had when
we took the Passover together there in the upper room.
How could it be? Wasn't he lying dead in some cold tomb?
His face said, "No." His eyes smiled, "Yes." How he got there, we
　　could not guess.

33

But, it was him. Of that, I'm sure. Though, once we recognized
    him,
he disappeared. He — poof! — was gone; the thin air just dis-
    guised him
and swallowed him up. We wished he'd stayed and talked with us
    a while,
but since he'd gone, we knew that we must cross these seven miles.
A miracle is what we saw. Only a miracle would explain it all!

I know what it is you're thinking; we're tired, with grief raw,
but none of that can completely explain the things we saw.
It was more than mere sight; it was vision so deep.
When he spoke of the scriptures, we followed like sheep.
Wisdom woke us with a start, and soon those words burned in our
    hearts.

Dead we were, our spirits slain. Through this teaching, we revived.
So, that moment in the broken bread was less of a surprise
than the completion of a process, a confirmation of the dream.
What the women said before was true! With joy, I had to scream!
I woke the children; scared the horse. But, that doesn't really mat-
    ter, of course!

So, here we stand, dust head to toe, but sure that it's all true.
He did not leave us, never will. Soon we'll know what we're to do.
Mary, Joanna, Salome, to all of you we apologize.
Your bravery, I do commend. You surely knew we'd close our eyes.
Foolish lies, we thought you'd told. But faithful to him, you were
    bold!

That's more than I can say for us. From Gethsemane, we ran.
And so did you, and you, and you. You weren't there at the end.
Yet, we're here, now. Together again. I don't know what that means,
except we knew there was something more before we'd seen these
    things.
Yes, we're thrilled that he's alive. But, what comes next, will we
    survive?

I'm talking crazy. I'm up and down, emotions bright and dark.
The truth is right before us and the light it shines is stark.
If he rose, as he said, then all that he said and did must be true!
Anointed one, and Son of God — yet, we're human through and
    through.
Seven miles of miracle we've crossed. But, one step more and I
    would be lost.

Well, I suppose we could clean up, so our company you'll stand.
Is there water here? Oh, yes, I see. Wait up, I'll give you a hand.
I need to wash, to feel the wetness take away the grime.
Would that mere water could cleanse the sin of abandoning him
    that time!
When I see him come again, I know, I must confess to be made
    whole.

What? My Lord, you're here again. You see, he's here. It's true!
Oh, yes, O Christ, you bring us peace. Peace be with you, too.
Huh? Of course we all believe. We're stunned, but we rejoice!
Fish, you want? Then, fish you'll have. *(to another)* Go on, you
    hear his voice.
But, first, there's something I must say. I ran, when they took you
    away.

I ... yes, I see. It's no surprise. You know my cowardice.
All I can say is "I repent!" But, do you know what I wish?
I wish I could replay that night and let them take me, too.
Then, there would be one, if only one, who walked that road with you.
Instead, you walked our road today. Why is it that you came our way?

(pause to hear his assurance)

So, love it is, a love so real you'd walk that road again.
Despite our sin, you love us still, and count us all as friends.
O gracious Lord, I humbly bow my heart to your command.
Never will I run again. With you, I die or stand.
Now, I'd best reign in my tongue, so you can tell us why you've
    come.

Throw It To The Dogs!

Making It Preach

Jesus' gift of salvation was for all nations, *beginning from Jerusalem* (Luke 24:47b). Yet, it must be claimed boldly with faith, whether by Jesus' own people or others. This woman's willingness to humbly, yet boldly demonstrate faith in his power became an opportunity for Jesus to point that out. His usage of the common derogatory term for Gentiles, *dogs*, differentiated foreign nations from his own people to whom he was sent. His main goal was to redeem the "lost sheep of the house of Israel." Yet, his own compassion for those suffering and his desire for all to display true faith spurred him on to this act of healing and his compliment regarding her great faith. The Roman centurion of Matthew 8:5-13 was another example of a foreigner whose faith surpassed that of many in Israel. Therefore, this Canaanite woman of Syrophoenician birth encourages the listeners to recognize their own need for Christ's saving grace and to boldly call upon his mercy in faith.

Making It Play

Strong-willed, somewhat rebellious, and focused on what her daughter needs: that is Ashrie's mother. She is one of those women who you either love or hate, but secretly admire, regardless. However, be careful that her tough exterior does not hide how she was affected by the very real pain and humiliation she experienced. That makes her current joy fuller and it makes the sudden humility of her words and actions before Jesus more obviously of divine origin. She would probably lack a head covering and may wear something non-traditional as a way of differentiating herself from an oppressive culture. Yet, faithful obedience should also come through as she refers to how she now serves Jesus by sharing her story.

A Mother Gladly Laps Up The Crumbs
That Fall From Jesus' Table

"Spunky!" I always liked that one, but most of the time it was just plain "stubborn," "willful," or even "mouthy!" My poor mom didn't know what to do with me, and my dad bounced back and forth between being amused and getting completely fed up with me. I guess they loved me in their way, but I was constantly embarrassing them, gaining the reputation as "the girl that doesn't know her place." Never mind that such behavior in boys was considered "spirited" and a sign of "strength of character"! Maybe if I had been born 2,000 years later, things would have been different, but I guess that just wasn't meant to be. Most people saw my *spunkiness* as some kind of a disability, as something I should be ashamed of. But, it ended up saving our lives!

Oh, I'm putting the cart before of the horse, here ... let's see. Where should I begin? Okay ... despite my parents' predictions to the contrary, there was a man who asked for my hand in marriage. He thought I was funny and full of life. He's the one who called me "spunky." He was a bit of a rebel, too, and my parents probably wouldn't have agreed to the match if they weren't so desperate for someone to marry me and get me off their hands. You see, my husband just traveled around from village to village, doing odd jobs here and there, never staying in one place for very long. Unfortunately, when I decided to surprise him by following him on one of his excursions, I found that I was not his only wife. So, I took off, after giving him several pieces of my mind, and my parents were stuck with me, once again. They didn't even try the speech about how "men will be men"; I have to give them credit for that.

I usually don't talk about him. I wish I could just erase that part of my life, except that it gave me the greatest gift I have ever received, my daughter, Ashrana. She's beautiful; of course, I'm biased as any mother worth her salt should be! Her laughter always made me stop feeling sorry for myself, stop caring about the scorn of others. You see, I had brought shame upon my family. They tried not to blame me, since they knew it wasn't really my fault that my marriage had been a joke, and I think most of them believed that, at least most of the time. But, the reality remained; I was a woman with a child and no husband. I was an alien in my hometown, a recipient of charity under the same roof that saw me grow up. I'd walk down the street and neighbors who once called out a "Hello!" whispered together as they passed me by. Once or twice, I whispered back, and not nearly so quietly, but eventually I just started to ignore them.

I'd make up all kinds of games to play with my little Ashrie, because I knew the other children weren't allowed to play with her. In fact, many of them had been taught to fear her because of her condition. Some said that it was because I had been a wicked woman, disobedient to my husband, that the gods cursed my Ashrie with a demon that attacked her, sometimes so severely that it took her hours to recover. Well, you want to know my answer to that? If their gods were responsible for that, then they can take their gods and ... I'll stop there because there are children in the room, but I think you get my point. Religious I have never professed to be, and that, of course, gave people even more reason to take pot shots.

But, believe it or not, I've actually come to you to share some good news, not my tale of woe. I told you that my spunkiness saved our lives, and it all began with a stranger who accidentally wandered through town. I say accidentally because no Jew would travel through here if he knew where he was going. We aren't exactly on the way to anywhere important, and Jews are even lower than me in most villagers' minds. After I saw him try to ask directions of a couple of people who spat in his face, I felt sorry for him and called him over. He didn't quite know what to make of me, at first, since men of his nation would only be approached by a woman if she was a prostitute or a beggar. And, here I was, not looking like either one, as far as he could tell, just trying to help him out. Once he decided to throw all caution to the wind, being desperately lost, we had quite a chat.

His name was Jesse, and he told me he was heading toward the Jewish settlement in Tyre because he heard that a great teacher and healer was moving in that direction. I was politely skeptical at first, "Are you sure he really fed thousands of people with a few loaves of bread and a couple of fish?" "Calmed a storm, did he?

How interesting!" But, when he got to the healing stuff, something snapped inside of me, especially when he said that this teacher named Jesus even healed the servant of a Roman centurion, the captors of the Jews, and our captors, too. It was like something inside of me popped and a big block of ice started to melt. Before I could stop it, I started to hope. If this Jesus would heal the servant of one of his nation's most dire enemies, why not my daughter? At least she had never pointed a spear at any of his people!

"I have to go with you!" I told him, which was the last thing Jesse wanted, but since I was the one who knew how to get there, he didn't have much choice. I ran in to tell my mother, who looked thoroughly confused, kissed my Ashrie on the forehead, and swore to her that I would not return until she was healed. That was a bit rash, I suppose, but you know how it is when the adrenaline starts pumping! I was so determined that I grew impatient with my companion when he wanted to stop for water. It was a two-day journey, and I had to make it there before the teacher moved on. He was my only hope.

I didn't even bother to clean myself up from the journey. When I finally saw him, I just called out, "Lord, Son of David, have mercy on me!" That was what I was told had worked for a blind man. "My daughter is suffering terribly from demon-possession!" Now, I have to admit, my first impression of this man was not the greatest. He appeared to be totally exhausted, and so when he looked at me, he just rolled his eyes, shook his head, and continued on down the road. But, I hadn't come all that way for nothing! So, I kept after him until, finally, his disciples told him to say something to get rid of me because I was giving them a headache. "Good!" I thought. That is nothing compared with what my daughter suffers every day!

So, he turned and mumbled over his shoulder, "I was sent only to the lost sheep of the house Israel." I was about to mention that Roman's servant, but I decided that, being a woman, the pathetic approach might be more effective. So, I dove in front of him, so he couldn't go forward, and bowing down, I begged him, "Lord, help me!" He stared at me with an expression I couldn't read, and I'm pretty good at telling what people are thinking. After a few seconds of silence in which I was certain he could hear the beating of my heart, he simply said, "It is not right to take the children's food and throw it to the dogs." Now, ordinarily, someone who said that to me would have been down in the dirt with me! But, I don't know if it was because I was so used to being insulted, or if I truly felt there was no malice behind his words, but I looked up into his eyes and saw that he was waiting for something.

"This is my chance!" I thought, maybe my only chance. And, I found myself doing something I had never done in my life. There, in a mixture of desperation and longing, I silently cried out three words to a God I had never even heard about until three days before. "God, save her!" And, then, as an afterthought. "God, save us!" Then, before I knew what I was saying, the words came flying out, words far more humble, and clever, than I could have come up with on my own. "Yes, Lord, yet even the dogs eat the crumbs that fall from their masters' table." Was I calling myself a dog?

But, before I could really think about that, a smile lit up his face and took away all of the creases of exhaustion. "Woman, great is your faith!" Me? "Let it be done for you as you wish," he told me, touched my arm, smiling (something that told me this guy was a bit of a "rebel," too!), and continued on.

I was stunned ... So was Jesse! I don't know who grabbed whose hand, but he fell on his knees beside me and, together, we praised the God who created the heavens and the earth, the only God, a God of mercy and love. Jesse promised to thank the healer as soon as he got the opportunity, so that I could return to my Ashrie. There was no question in my mind about the truth of his statement. She was healed!

What are you thinking? Let me guess: *Oh, that's a nice story*, right? But, what has that got to do with you? Well, I'll tell you, as I have been telling all kinds of folks ever since that miraculous day. You can get the demons out of your life, too! What demons? Oh, don't think I am so naive. You know where they lurk, how they bring you shame, how they disrupt your life and separate you from others, and even your God. I can't tell you what they are. Maybe the only one who can is that healer who saved our lives,

41

mine and Ashrana's, because I saw things in his eyes during those brief seconds I might never have uncovered. No, you can't actually look into his eyes; he's moved on now. But, if you pray in your heart, you will know him just the same. It takes some courage because he sees all of who you are, but he can release you and those you love from the things that otherwise might destroy you. Go ahead; don't be afraid. If he will heal foreigners like my daughter and me, and the servant of that Roman centurion, he will heal you, too!

Oh, my daughter's calling. Remember, crying out, "Son of David, have mercy on me!" really works. Throw yourselves down before him, and it is amazing who you might become before you rise again. Let it be so, my friends.

Hatching The Golden Rule

Making It Preach

It is easy for us to forget that Jesus was comparing us with the unmerciful servant, not the king nor the one the servant would not forgive. Thus it is in the kingdom of heaven, Jesus comments before this parable. He shared this story to remind his followers that not forgiving one who wrongs us is like trampling God's immeasurable gift of mercy in the dirt. The concluding verse of Matthew 18 warns that God does not take such disrespect lightly. Yet, Jesus gave us the way to avoid God's wrath, *Repent, for the kingdom of heaven has come near* (Matthew 4:17). Our storyteller provides us with a small example of what that means. She confesses her own sin to God and stops misusing her power as a corporate vigilante. Instead, she tells Christ's story, giving God the credit for truly setting things right. She repents and seeks to right her sinful lack of mercy and reminds the congregation to do the same.

Making It Play

Business attire and an attitude of confidence and almost arrogant competence make up this woman's ensemble. She should be played slightly larger-than-life to become a fun and inventive storyteller. As 9/11 and the Enron collapse fade into the history books, feel free to choose more contemporary examples of stock market instability and corporate corruption. Do not be afraid to add some pretend gun slinging and any other bits of playacting this woman might use to make her story more dramatic. But, her final plea to the congregation should be sincere and filled with concern for the listeners.

The Parable Of The Unmerciful Servant
Given A Modern Twist

Hey! What are you looking at? You think that just because I come out of the Bible I have to wear a tunic and sandals? I'll tell you something, I get mighty tired of that *having to keep my hair covered* rule. Besides, since Jesus told parables using settings with which the people were familiar, you are the very people who need to recognize me, today — and I don't see any of you ladies wearing a heavy, old cloth on your heads!

Who am I? Just call me "Jacki-of-all-Trades." I answer phones, respond to email, run to Starbucks, do the newsletter, get the company cars washed, and anything else the big muckety-mucks ask me to do. I'm invaluable precisely because I'm flexible; if a job doesn't fit into anyone else's job description, it gets added to mine. My job description is currently almost four pages long. Now, that's what I call job security! Talking with you folks today is yet another facet of what I do; it is the most important facet, one I know inside and out. In fact, if I stopped doing it, I would have to cease to exist, and I have never been one to blend quietly into the background! So, sit back, relax, but not too much — if I notice any of you sleeping, I might just have to box you on the ears! You see, I've got a story to tell.

In this company, we had an ambitious bookkeeper named Ted who always had a smile on his face and a scheme in his heart. He was always trying to impress the higher-ups with one ingenious plan after another, swearing each one would save the company thousands of dollars per year, per quarter, per month! And, most of the time, they would patiently smile, nod, and pay absolutely no attention to what he was saying. So, he decided to take matters into his own hands; matters, may I add, that he had no authority touching with a ten-foot pole! He switched some numbers around, set up a phony account, and diverted a huge chunk of change into an investment portfolio he was sure would make big bucks, and then he'd be rewarded with some colossal promotion. Well, he did this over time, finishing up somewhere around September 10, 2001 — are you starting to get the picture, here? I even asked him if he'd lost somebody in the 9/11 tragedy, since his ever-present smile became forced and he looked worse and worse every day. "No, no — I'm just a little under the weather, that's all. Don't worry, nothing keeps me down for long!" he'd answer, making a lame attempt at enthusiasm.

Now, he was pretty clever at covering things up, but by year-end, it became obvious that our profits could not have plunged as much as the figures were showing. At audit time, they finally put their fingers on the leak and our little Dutch boy found himself with a lot of explaining to do. Yep! He was on his way up ... as in, up the elevator to the floors where the big bosses have their offices, and he found himself in the wigwam of the C.F.O., Big Chief Finance Officer! Okay, I'll admit I did not have any specific reason to be on that floor at that time ... but I came up with one! And, let me tell you, Little Scout went into the biggest sob story you've ever heard about how his mother was diagnosed with cancer, but had no insurance, and his wife was having difficulty with her pregnancy. He just knew that if somebody noticed him, he had so much to offer the company at higher levels of responsibility, which would also allow him to take care of his family's needs, blah-blah-blah-blah-blah.

And, you know something? Little Scout is quite an actor, and Big Chief was drawn into the performance. Yep, I got the whole scoop from one of my many sources! Big Chief was moved to show more compassion in that one case than I had seen him display in all the years I've worked here! They sat down and talked about ways to do damage control, which wouldn't be easy after the Enron collapse, and then they worked out a plan for Little Scout to work off a percentage of the money they had lost — work it off! That little weasel didn't even get fired! Now, granted, if his mother was really that ill and his wife and baby were in trouble, I didn't want to see them hurt by his arrogance. But, I found myself just shaking my head as Buddy-boy joined me in the elevator heading back down. "What?" he asked. I just gave him an innocent shrug.

I'll tell you, though my impression of the C.F.O. as a brilliant business shark was tainted a bit, I found I liked him a lot more. But, my initial impressions of Ted the bookkeeper soon proved to be frighteningly astute. Ted acted with forced humility for a few days, but it didn't take long for his true nature to come shining through. Jim, who is part of our maintenance crew and a great guy (he'd do anything to help you out!), went to Ted one morning and explained that he'd accidentally run into Ted's car in the parking lot. It had just started to rain and the pavement was slippery, but the recently forgiven cowboy was not in a forgiving mood. I like to read action stories — so, sue me! Anyway, he demanded Jim's insurance card, and when Jim explained that his insurance had lapsed because he was low on money, but that he would pay the repair off as soon as he could, Ted pulled out the big guns. Half the people on the floor heard him; I think he wanted them to hear him, to draw attention to Jim's carelessness and make him feel about this *(indicate with fingers)* big. Ted declared that his car was a collector's model and that if Jim did not pay him off immediately, he would turn him in for having no insurance and take him to small claims court, seeking to bilk him for as much in the way of extra damages as he could muster.

I was appalled! How could that little snake escape the eagle's talons by such a narrow margin and then turn around and sink his fangs into Jim? What a creep! Now, I'll admit I didn't have any specific reason to take my distraught self up to the floor of the big bosses ... but I thought of one. So, there I was, noticeably becoming unglued outside the C.F.O.'s office, when his assistant asked me what was wrong. I casually leaned against his desk and just happened to hit the intercom to the C.F.O.'s office as I explained the antics of the Little Serpent with a big bite! And, what do you know? Big Chief heard the whole story — oops! So, he quickly came out and had me repeat it, to make sure he was hearing me correctly. Ooo-ooh-eee! I think I actually heard him growl — I guess he didn't get to his position by always being Mr. Nice Guy! He looked at me, dead serious, and asked if anyone else could corroborate my story. "Sure," I told him, "ask anyone who was sitting within a fifty-foot radius!" Then, he got this little smile on his face, one of those that lets you know you better be ready to duck at the right time 'cause "something wicked this way comes." Then, he offered me his arm and asked if I would accompany him on a little "snake hunt." Okay, maybe that's not what he said, but I knew what he meant!

And, you know what? I found myself worrying about Ted's mother and wife and child-to-be, as the elevator made its quick descent. I started hoping against hope that he had made all that stuff up, that they wouldn't be hurt because of Snake Boy, there, and because I was the one who squealed on him! I found myself praying, asking God if I had done the right thing. Well, I'm still not sure about that, but I have a feeling that if I hadn't let the snake out of the bag, it would have come out some other way. Everybody likes Jim, so Ted didn't score many popularity points that day. I don't know, even if God was using my natural curiosity to bust this guy out, I still needed to confess my sin in making the way for revenge. "Vengeance is mine!" sayeth the Lord — not mine.

Well, as you could guess, fireworks exploded on the second floor! "I showed more mercy to you than I thought made good business sense because I felt sorry for you and your family. I gave you a break when I don't give breaks!" Big Chief's voice got louder and louder. "And, you have the gall to humiliate one of our most valuable employees because he accidentally made a boo-boo on your car?" Then, it was silent — it was kind of eerie. His voice became suddenly calm. "You'd better pack your things, Ted, because after I call security, I will be calling the C.E.O. and then the police! I hope you don't object to being confined in a small cell for a long, long time." When Ted opened his mouth to speak, the Chieftain gave him a look that would douse a fire and marched down the hall with the purpose of the president on his way to a national security briefing.

No, it wasn't exactly any old day around the office. It sure showed me what can happen when you don't follow the Golden Rule. Next time you are tempted to not "do unto others as you'd have them do unto you," you might want to remember this Parable of the Unmerciful Servant, I mean, Bookkeeper. You see, before Jesus told this parable, Peter, his right hand man, thought he was being pretty generous — like he was going to impress Jesus by offering to forgive his brother as many as seven times. Well, Jesus

47

said that doesn't even begin to cover it, if you look at how many times God forgives us! Big Chief was generous once, really generous, but as soon as he got his buns burned, he turned nasty. And, most of us know that we would not even be here if that were how God decided to operate. But, by God's mercy in giving us Jesus, we are given a second chance, then a third, and a fifth, and a 105th on down the line.

Sure, there are people who just trip our triggers, and sometimes it may seem that teaching them a lesson would have a much better effect on them than biting our tongues and forgiving them. They deserve a dose of their own medicine, don't they? But, truthfully, the same could be said about us. "Oh, Pharmacist! Cancel that prescription." Anyone want to join me? It starts right here *(point to cross)*.

Proper 26 / Pentecost 24 / Ordinary Time 31
Joshua 3:1-17

Cross Over Or Cross Out

Making It Preach

This piece compares the physical crossing of the Jordan River
and all of its religious implications for the people of Israel with
what it means for a person to cross over into the arms of Jesus.
Miriam's granddaughter remembers that momentous day, feeling
the incredible import of being a link between two acts of God's
deliverance, the exodus and the entrance into the promised land.
Through Jesus, those events are part of every Christian's heritage,
and as our troubadour points out, it is our turn to tell the tale and
add how God's salvation story continues in our lives, individually
and corporately. Her grandmother Miriam's song from Exodus
15:21 invites a new generation of those who have received God's
grace to rejoice in and tell of the ways Christ continues to bring
people over and through the armies of opposition and the sea of
separation from God.

Making It Play

It is important to allow the rhythm of the poetry to add flow
without getting in the way of the story. Do not automatically pause
at the end of a line if the sentence continues to the middle of the
next. Though it may take a little while for the listeners' ears to
adjust to the verse, they will soon feel the excitement and range of
emotion recounted by Miriam's granddaughter. Make up a tune
for Miriam's song, if you have the gift of music. If not, chant the
words with reverence and perhaps clap or march to suggest a beat.
A simple tunic with head covering is sufficient externally, but make
sure the awe and conviction of one trying to describe a miracle
bubbles up from within.

Miriam's Granddaughter Recounts The Miracle
Of Entering The Promised Land

The dust arose. The day had come.
The ark came forth to lead us home,
gleaming gold topped angel's wings,
a throne, but not for earthly kings.
Yet, there it shone right through the haze of sand kicked up around.
We sat on pins and needles, hoping to hear the footsteps sound.

For Joshua had put out the word,
confirming what we'd always heard:
that someday when our parents died
we'd cross over to the other side
of the Jordan. What a river! "Could a land of promise lie
beyond your banks?" we'd sit and wonder. "What's the treasure
     that you hide?"

"Pack up your things!" The cry went out.
I couldn't tell, amid the shouts,
why we had to move again.
Please, not another grievous sin!
My people's stubborn nature is like the grit between my teeth.
So, the punishment continues. Will we ever find release?

I'm tired of the nomad way;
it's all I've known day after day.
Moving, stopping, off we go —
I want *one* place to call a home.
Perhaps, I'm wrong. Perhaps I'd become bored with just one spot.
But, I'd love the chance to try it, whether I'd want that life or not!

As these thoughts swirled through my mind,
I felt a nudge come from behind.
"Did you hear?" My little sister tugged
my clothing, then my waist she hugged.
"We're going there! We're going there!" I had to ask, "We're go-
     ing where?"

"The promised land — we're going home! There's not much time,
        but I don't care!"

She ran ahead and spun around.
But, I was rooted to the ground.
We're going in? Could it be true?
There's so much that we have to do!
But, if she's wrong, my heart will break! Did her hopes eclipse her
        hearing?
Dare I believe it's happening? It was a letdown I was fearing,

the loss of a precious dream,
the dulling of fabled gleam.
Would the Lord change the plan,
again keep us from the land
if someone messes up today? Let them put their pride aside!
Lord, help them trust in something bigger, not themselves, but you,
        their guide!

Thus, I prayed, for three days straight,
and, oh, it was so hard to wait!
But, as I said before: that day,
that day, it took my breath away!
When the priests brought forth the ark to lead us and we all fell in
        behind,
a new life stretched out before us, almost too much for the mind.

Pa-dum, pa-dum, the sound of feet,
pa-dum, pa-dum, the blistering heat
I barely felt, as we walked.
No one even dared to talk.
It was as if we held our breath along the path to the river.
There were no questions of how we'd cross; its mere sight made
        me shiver.

Oh, river of freedom, servant of sin,
you river that once fenced us in

will split, I know, as did the Red Sea.
You'll open up for what's to be,
the path I've yet to trod. Pa-dum, pa-dum, our feet, they padded
along.
Shall I be another Miriam there, to sing and play the victory song?

Her daughter was my mother, so
it's fitting I prepare to go
and play her tune and sing her song.
That way, she will go along
with me and see what her brother Moses saw from atop the
mountain's peak.
Though they perished on the journey, those slaves will reach the
land they seek.

Ready to cross, not just ourselves,
but a people of the twelve
tribes of Israel, Jacob's clan,
born and blessed by God's hand.
Since Jacob's time our favor died, Egypt's wealth to Egypt's chains
to dirt and manna, grit and greed. But, our hope in the Lord is alive
again.

Have you ever been part of a miracle,
to stand in awe with a heart that's full
and a spirit in touch with the Spirit of the Lord?
I'd give away more than I could afford
to recapture that magic moment, when the Jordan's waters ceased
to flow.
The priests with the ark set their feet in the water; a pathway dried
up and the bottom showed!

Then in we marched, again holding our breath,
feeling one false move could end in death.
Yet, deeper still, inside we knew
we needn't fear God's promise true.

And, so we reached the other shore, the edges of the promised
    land,
where milk and honey and fertile fields would soon replace the
    barren sand.

So, here we are, and here we'll stay.
Wilderness fading, a new day awaits,
but first there are battles that need to be won.
There is nothing new under the sun.
An easier life we were promised, yes, but an easy life will never
    be.
Still, I have my grandmother's song to sing, a song of triumph o'er
    the sea.

"Sing ye to the Lord,
for he hath triumphed gloriously:
the horse and his rider
hath he thrown into the sea.
Sing ye to the Lord,
for he hath triumphed gloriously.
Alleluia! Alleluia!"

There are other verses I could write,
of tears and struggle and faith in flight,
of a river crossing and a brand new land,
the fulfillment of promise at the Lord's strong hand.
But, you could write more, so many more words, about the people
    of promise saved for your sake
and the Messiah who loved you and gave of his life to make the
    way for your escape.

What is it you sing? What's the story you tell:
despair and deliverance ... salvation, as well?
Have you yet to cross over, or is the crossing now done?
How much farther will you go? Will that race you run?
Please — make up a song or a rhyme or just speak from your heart
    to your friends.

Tell of the journey of faith you have walked and share how that
    journey never ends.

Invite them to come, if they dare;
it will be a sign that you care.
They are far less likely to haw and hem
if you promise you will walk with them.
Or, maybe you need them to walk with you, much as my people
    fell into step
and crossed together, and fought for our place, as the Lord's great
    plan and promise were kept.

You sing your song, and I'll sing mine.
And, together, our God we will glorify.
"Sing ye to the Lord
for he hath triumphed gloriously:
the horse and his rider
hath he thrown into the sea.
Sing ye to the Lord
for he hath triumphed gloriously.
Alleluia! Alleluia!"
Amen.

Left In The Dark

Making It Preach

Though this parable points out that we know neither the day nor hour the bridegroom (named Jesus) will return, we are admonished to be ready. With the exception of small groups of Christians some might call fanatics, contemporary Christians have lost the sense of urgency our ancestors in the faith felt regarding Christ's return. We figure he has already been gone so long that the likelihood of his return during our lifetime is pretty low. Yet, as our bridesmaid friend points out, the amount of unfinished business many of us face could take quite a long time to sort through and correct. We must also remember the point Jesus made in his story about the man who decided to build bigger barns to store his wealth for the future — there may be no future (Luke 12:16-21). Death could bring us before Jesus at any moment — will our hearts and minds be ready? Will evidence of our faith and eagerness be there when Jesus comes to invite us to his eternal feast?

Making It Play

In the days before movies, ball games, and laser tag, weddings were a welcome form of entertainment, especially the multiple-day festivities often celebrated during Jesus' time. The bridesmaids had to wait due to the custom of the bridegroom collecting his bride from her parents' home and bringing her to his for the celebration. This bridesmaid could adorn herself with a fancy tunic and head covering that makes her look young and ready for the special occasion she just missed, or she could simply treat this as a memory and wear a simple tunic and head covering. If it would be more believable for this to be a memory from her girlhood, go ahead and fit that into the story. Either way, the exuberance of youth should be heard in her voice as she tells the story. If you have a Middle Eastern clay lamp, please use it for reference. However, it would be better to pantomime than to use a more modern western lamp.

A "Foolish" Bridesmaid
Presents Her Side Of The Story

Then the kingdom of heaven will be like this. Ten bridesmaids took their lamps and went to meet the bridegroom. Five of them were foolish, and five were wise (Matthew 25:1-2). Now, Jesus may have made us up in his head and everything, but I think it was a little hasty to call some of us *foolish*. He could have said we were not-too-prepared that night, or maybe we were just go-with-the-flow kinds of gals, but foolish? I don't think I like that. Let me give you another side of the story.

Life had gotten really boring around our village: get up, do some chores, make a meal, do some more chores, make another meal, lay down, get up and do more chores ... I mean a girl needs a little excitement now and then. But one day, we found out that the agreement was made. My cousin, Zach, would be marrying Leah, the daughter of Benjamin who oversees the vineyard. And, you know what that made the young people around here think about? It's time to party! I love to dance, and when we have a wedding feast, it is nothing like those private one-day little affairs you have in your country. The entire village and surrounding community is invited, and it usually goes on for days. It would be pretty hard not to get caught up in the excitement. The smells of good food and freshly washed garments, preparations in the village square — you know, even though it means more work to get everything ready, nobody seems to mind because we finally have something fun to think about. Even the elders, who try to look so serious most of the time, smile as much as anyone else during the wedding feasts!

So, you're wondering about that night, aren't you? You're probably asking why, if I was so excited about the celebration, I got shut out of the main feast? This is why. *(holds up a small clay lamp)* Not very big, I realize, but I grabbed it at the last minute. It had recently been filled with oil, so I figured it would burn long enough. How was I to know that Zach would be so long in picking up Leah and bringing her to the feast? They obviously weren't in a hurry! There were my sisters and I, and the other young women, dressed to kill, ready to dance and eat and check out the single men, and we waited, and waited, and ... well we'd been up since before the sun shone that morning doing chores and then getting ourselves ready, and most of us hadn't slept well because of all the excitement. So, we fell asleep. Finally, about midnight, shouts in the distance woke us up. We did our best to straighten ourselves up, and prepared ourselves to join the happy couple for one of those all-night-long parties.

Then, I looked down, and my lamp started flickering. I thought it might have been the wind, but then I realized, there wasn't any wind. "Wouldn't you know?" I thought to myself. I wanted to ignore the fact that my lamp was running out of oil, but my eldest sister Mariah was watching me like a hawk, *bless her heart!*, and said I had better get more oil, pronto. You see, it's not like we had street lighting to help us out. No lamps means you can't see anything when the moon is waning. "You could trip and dirty your clothes," Mariah in all her wisdom told me. Because her voice is less than quiet, all the others looked at me, then the same thing was pointed out to a few of my friends who also brought no extra oil with them.

"Come on, give us a little of yours," I begged, "it can't be that much longer." But, it was like talking to stone walls.

"We don't have enough for all of us. You know where to buy it. Get your own!" Don't you just love sisterly compassion?

So, off we went, trying to walk as smoothly and quickly as possible so that we wouldn't run out of oil before we made it to the dealer. We could hear the laughing and shouting in the distance, and my first impulse was to say forget it and run to join them. However, if I got stuck in absolute darkness before I got to them, that would not have been a good thing. God was good and got us to the dealer's house before we had completely run out. One thing we hadn't counted on, however, was that he was fast asleep. Apparently, he didn't think he had too many midnight parties left in him, so we had to bang on his door and bang and bang! When he did open up, he was less-than-pleased to see us, and we really had to do some fast talking to get him to sell us some oil in the middle of the night. He was kind of grumpy and not real *with it*, since he'd just been awakened, so he took forever getting us the oil, all the while complaining about how tired he was and how he needed his rest for the festivities tomorrow and how grateful we should be that he was not going to just leave us in the dark. I looked at my friend Tabitha, and I could just tell she wasn't hearing a word he was saying, that instead she was trying to judge how far along the wedding procession was getting as we stood there.

Finally, we got on our way and took off at a quick pace, hoping to catch up with the procession before it reached the place of the feast. But, then, my sandal got caught on a rock and ripped. That was it! I didn't care anymore. I took off my sandals, we all did, and hurried as quickly as we could to the feast. By the time we found everyone, they were well into the party, the ceremony was about to begin, and our feet and the bottoms of our garments were pretty dirty. So, when Zach saw us about to enter, he took this attitude with us. I suppose he felt we didn't care about the celebration since we were late and didn't look so hot, so he said, "I do not know you," and he sent us away!

Not know us! After all we had gone through to get to that party, he sent us away! Can you believe that? One of the few chances for excitement in our lives, and we missed the best part because of this! *(holds up the lamp)* I was about to smash this little baby against a rock, but Tabitha stopped me, "Do that and we'll really be left in the dark! At least we've got a light to find our way home. That's something." I think I liked her better when she was a skinny little kid who didn't say much, but she did have a point. On the way home, I was thinking about how excited I had been for weeks, and how the highlight of the whole shebang was soon going to be over, without me. It's funny how you can start out so excited, get yourself busy preparing for the feast, dream of what it will be like to celebrate, but when the time comes, you find out you haven't prepared well at all.

I guess that's what Jesus was trying to warn you about by calling us *foolish.* Only, since you have electricity, he was talking about your faith, not your oil, how your faith in God and your enthusiasm for God could run out before Jesus returns to take you from this life to be with him forever. If I didn't have time to get more oil, how are you going to have time to get things right with God and clean up the messes in your life? How will you clear up that misunderstanding with your son or coworker? How are you going to make up for all you didn't do for the old lady across the street? How are you going to say you are sorry to all the people you hurt or cheated? How are you going to get yourselves ready with so much left undone? It takes time to clean them up and you don't know how much time you have. I am part of Jesus' imagination and I even don't know that! But, like Tabitha said, you do have a light to lead you home. Jesus himself gives you a light by letting you know how to clean up your sins and turn to God, and God, unlike my cousin, will take you in even without shoes or if you're dirty and tattered. You just need to be ready to turn to God, with a heart that has dealt with regrets and mistakes and is ready to move on. And, if I could do it again, I'd do everything I could to arrive at the feast on time, rested, clean, and determined to celebrate. I told you I'm not foolish ... at least not anymore! *Shalom.*

Year B

Dear John

Making It Preach

After all the talk, the first step of walking the walk is repentance. This John the Baptist groupie has not murdered anyone, committed adultery, stolen valuable property; neither have most Christians. But, she does come to the realization that even a relatively small secret sin can keep her from fully opening her heart to God. Having repented and been given the assurance of God's love for her, the waters of baptism wash her clean in a mighty rush of grace. No matter how far along one is on the Christian journey, it is crucial to periodically return to the river to be cleansed and to reclaim new life in Christ. *Therefore we have been buried with him by baptism into death, so that, just as Christ was raised from the dead by the glory of the Father, so we too might walk in the newness of life* (Romans 6:4).

Making It Play

Remember falling in love with a teacher, heart throb actor, or rock star? The unreachable factor does not discourage fantasies of a great romance. Draw upon the giddy, emotion-packed memories and act accordingly: Age does not necessarily make much difference in how these feelings play themselves out. John has had that effect on this new believer, who epitomizes the term *starry-eyed.* She does not realize that some of her feelings derive from the joyful release from guilt and shame that repentance brings. She just rides the euphoria and uncertainty and attributes them to John. She may play with her head covering rather than wearing it, as she lets the congregation in on her agonizing, tantalizing secret.

Can She Break The Baptist's Heart
After He Has Cleansed Hers?

(enters, singing a bit of Gene Pitney's classic, "He's A Rebel")

Oh, who am I kidding? He doesn't even know I exist. Nevertheless, things cannot go on as they are. His wardrobe is deplorable, though in a rugged, manly sort of way. Camel's hair is definitely rugged. But, I can't invite him to my parents' house for a nice, kosher sabbath meal dressed like that! And, his eating habits ... now, I have nothing against exotic, and wild honey sounds exotic and succulent, but locusts? I can just see my mother beginning the sabbath prayers when John's hand swoops up, grabs a moth, and pops it into his mouth as an appetizer! No, this is never going to work. It's best if I just end it now, even if it never really started.

I'll have to send a message to him. What should it say? "Dear John ..." Oh, how could I do this? He'll be crushed! Under all that ranting and raving, John is a very sensitive man. I could tell from the moment I looked into his eyes. "Sister, do you repent of your sins?" That is what he said when I first saw him in the Jordan River, none of that *nice weather we're having* small talk for him, no sir, he went straight to the point. Or, maybe straight to the heart would be a better way of saying it, straight to my heart. You see, I had been thinking a lot about my sins ever since my cousin, Andrew, came back one day and said that he'd been baptized by John in the Jordan after repenting.

"What's repenting?" I asked. Girls weren't allowed to go to the classes with the rabbi, so I was kind of behind on all that religious stuff.

"It means you have to turn away from your sins and turn back to God, Stu ..." He was about to call me *Stupid*, but then he remembered that he had just repented and been baptized and all that. It seemed to me like a big improvement in Andrew, and trust me, there was plenty of room for improvement!

So, I decided to start thinking about my own sins. I went through the Ten Commandments, like a quiz, seeing how I'd come out. Actually, I was doing pretty well. I run around a bit too much on the sabbath. I did take my sister's bracelet once, but I felt so guilty, I gave it back right away. Never mind that she has three of them, and I don't have any! I haven't blamed anybody for something they didn't do since I was about five years old. Yeah, I was doing well until I got to that last commandment about not coveting. Whew! I really blew it there. Ever since we were small and I pushed her down to get her new skirt dirty, I have been jealous of my sister. Her beautiful complexion and eyes, her laugh, her graceful walk, and her ability to charm anyone, even Andrew, into doing things for her ... I wanted it all! I would criticize her when she was around (only, subtly, so my parents wouldn't notice), then, when she was gone, I would try to be like her. My mother noticed that! So, she took a break from baking one day, grabbed me by the arm, and led me to the field across from our house.

"Look at the flowers," she said. "Which is the prettiest?" I looked at them all, and just as I was about to make a selection, another one would catch my eye, then another.

Finally, I just told her, "They are all pretty in their own way. I don't think I could choose."

"Neither can God. Smell your own fragrance. It's lovely." That's all she said, and she turned around and hurried back inside to her bread.

Unfortunately, I didn't get it, not until I did the Ten Commandment thing. But, even when I realized it, I knew I couldn't just change how I felt like *that*, at least not by myself. So, I swallowed my pride and went down to where Andrew was mending his nets. I asked if that John guy baptized females, too. He said he saw all kinds of people, men and women, at the river that day. So, it was decided. I just needed to come up with a good excuse to get out of my chores, which Andrew had no trouble making up, and I was off to the river.

As I stood there in line, my confidence dwindled. What if I get up there and that holy man just looks at me and goes, "Forget it. You're hopeless!" But, then I heard his voice, John's voice calling out clear and strong, "Prepare the way of the Lord! Make his paths straight!" Suddenly, I was filled with this desire to prepare my heart for the coming of the Messiah. But, before I could ask how,

John seemed to answer my question. "Repent for the kingdom of heaven is near!"

Andrew's words echoed through my head. "It means you have to turn away from your sins and turn back to God."

"Okay, God," I prayed. "I think I'm ready. I don't want to stay in the shadows, trying to steal my sister's sunshine."

Then, as if he heard my prayer, the man standing next to me turned and told me about how, on the previous day, John baptized the one he said was to be the Messiah. And, when he was baptized, the heavens opened and a voice said, "This is my beloved Son. With him, I am well pleased."

"You are his beloved daughter," he suddenly said to me. "Take heart." I quickly glanced at John, and when I looked back at the stranger, he was gone. But, his words did something to my heart. I felt free. I felt loved. I was ready to repent of my sins and turn back to the God who created and loves me. I was ready to be plunged into those muddy waters and emerge, smelling my own fragrance, and loving it!

Then, I heard John preaching, "I baptize you with water, but the one who comes after me will baptize you with the Holy Spirit and with fire!" From the way my heart was burning, I had a feeling that the one coming after him had been the one standing next to me, reassuring me that I, too, was precious in God's sight.

The next thing I knew, it was my turn to be baptized, and that's when I first saw John's eyes and melted. His voice was rich and gentle. "Sister, do you repent of your sins?" All I could do was nod. *(nods, in love)* And then, he touched me. He put his strong fingers on my scarf, and I wanted that touch to last forever. Then, his grip got firmer, and he plunged my head into the water so fast that my scarf flew off and I got water up my nose! But, then he pulled me out into the sunshine before you could say *John the Baptist* and overall, it was a rather exhilarating experience — except for the water up my nose! It was all over so quickly. By the time I had cleared my nose, wiped my eyes, and found my scarf, John was already plunging the next person into the cloudy deep. But, I knew I would never forget him.

Now, Andrew and I share something profound. Go figure! That is something I never would have dreamed could be possible! Andrew is even one of John's disciples, now. I have been wanting to go back to the river to rekindle our relationship, but practicality keeps stopping me ... and safety. You see, John's words cut at people's hearts and challenge them to really live out their faith, and that has annoyed a lot of the officials and even King Herod. What John says is the truth; it's a gift that God has given him. But, he'd better be careful how loudly he says it!

You know, with a good haircut and tailor, and definitely some lessons on mealtime etiquette, it might have worked. But, why does he have to be such a rebel? Oh well, I'd better figure out how to let him down easy. Pray for him, will you? And, I'll pray for you, that each of you will go to the river, and that your hearts will be pierced by his words so that the one who comes after John can get in and change your lives forever! You won't regret it!

(Walks off, singing "He's A Rebel")

Christmas 1
Luke 2:22-40

The Crazy One And The Chosen One

Making It Preach

This Gentile woman who, along with her husband, sells birds for sacrifice near the temple is truly an *outsider looking in*. Yet, we hear her yearning to belong to a god, the God, who will claim her as part of a diverse family. She hears in Simeon's prophetic words what today's Christians forget: Gentiles enlarged the Jewish roots of Christianity according to God's design, and being a ... *light for revelation to the Gentiles* ... (Luke 2:32) was part of Jesus' identity. Twenty-first-century Christians need to reflect upon who the modern day outsiders/Gentiles are and remember that Jesus came to save them, too. Since the church is Christ's incarnation now, being a light for revelation to folks on the outside must remain part of the church's identity and mission.

Making It Play

Our narrator's character is not clearly defined, since her story is of Anna, Simeon, and Jesus' parents. Take some time to decide how she should portray this: merchant, wife, seeker, or observer of human nature. Once the storyteller is defined, then she can focus on bringing the other characters alive through her telling. Her dress, though necessarily modest to be accepted in Jerusalem, could reflect foreign influence. The congregation might be addressed as if they are customers or fellow merchants who approach her booth.

Anna's Announcement About
The Messiah's Birth Attracts Attention

Did you see all of the excitement over there? Anna's all astir this morning. I don't think I've ever seen that much life in the old girl. Every morning early while my husband and I are out here setting up to sell our birds, we see Anna shuffle from her room to the temple of her God. And, we go home before she even comes out. From what I hear, she has been doing that as long as anybody can remember. A bit of an odd duck, I'd say, but she usually has a smile and a "hello" for us when she passes. Occasionally she'll purchase a bird or two from us for sacrifice, though she doesn't have much to spend. What she does have seems to come from good people who look out for her. Some even think she's a prophetess. Others call her crazy, but harmless. I suppose the line between the two isn't all that clear, anyway.

There she goes. She's like a woman on a mission. Standing at the gate to the outer court as people enter the temple, she's telling them about the redemption of Israel. Now, these Jews are always talking about that, I suppose because they don't have much else to look forward to with the Romans in charge, but Anna's adding a different twist. See, I decided to wander over there earlier when she was talking to some folks on a pilgrimage to the temple. She was trying to tell them that the Messiah they are always talking about has been born and that he was just dedicated in the temple a few days ago. Poor old Anna, though most of the people try to be polite, you can tell very few, if any, of them, believe her. They have been waiting so long for this Messiah, I guess they have given up on the hope that they'll ever really see him. One thing I do have to give her credit for is that she won't give up.

Okay, now Simeon's there, trying to back up her story, no doubt. Before, she was telling how something called the Holy Spirit had given Simeon a revelation that he would not die until he had seen this Messiah with his own eyes. Then, this Spirit apparently led Simeon to the temple on the day the parents of this promised child brought him to be dedicated, and he just knew that this was the one. I hear the parents looked just as shocked as everyone else when this old man came shuffling up to them and proclaimed that

70

their baby was the Savior of their people. My husband got the inside story from some others who were there at the time. Can you imagine it? This couple was rough, I hear, from some little village in Galilee. My husband sold them a couple of birds — pigeons or turtledoves, I forget which. From what I understand, that's the acceptable sacrifice for a firstborn male when you can't afford a lamb and a pigeon. Just picture it! They come to the big city to follow up on the rules of their religion regarding their baby, and suddenly they are accosted by Simeon, who starts a ruckus, praising God because their baby is going to be the consolation of Israel. Whew! Probably made them want to turn tail and run back home to the simple life! Then, Simeon supposedly told the mother that the consolation her son would bring wouldn't be without great upset and personal pain for her. Nice welcome to town!

There is one thing that Anna said about Simeon's rantings that interests me, though, since my husband and I come from another land. We just moved here about six years ago. Anna quoted Simeon as saying that this child would be a light for revelation to the Gentiles — that's their word for the rest of us who are not Jewish. I wonder what he meant by that. There are some foreigners who have taken up the practice of worshiping this Jewish God, but they are only allowed into the outermost court of the temple, and they still have to follow all the zillions of religious codes of the faith. I wonder, if this child is really who they say he is, does that mean he will open up the doors so that foreigners would have equal access to the God of Israel?

My husband and I don't worship the gods of our own people anymore since we are in a different land and those gods never seemed to do anything for us, even when we were at home. This God of Israel has always interested me; I'm curious by nature, so I ask a lot of questions. You see, this is the first god I've ever heard of who actually seems loyal to his or her own people even when they don't follow all of the rules and wander away, even in the midst of hard times. It has to do with this promise, or covenant they call it, that their god made to one of their ancestors. Some of their ancient prophets also talked about how this god would eventually be *the* God of the whole world, one day claiming people from every nation. *(whispers)* But, don't try and tell that to the officials here in the temple!

Anna doesn't even look tired. She's been standing there, prophesying some might say, for hours. She does have unusual energy today; she's no spring chicken, and I know my birds! She must really believe what she's saying. In a strange sort of way, I admire Anna more than anyone else I've seen or met around the temple, even the priests. Though few people really listen to her because she's a woman, I bet her god does. She faithfully prays every day; Anna doesn't just go through the motions of religion. Love for her god just oozes from her; it's in everything she does.

I wish I had that passion and sense of purpose in life. I've watched some really ridiculous rituals in my lifetime to all sorts of gods, and even though I think most of it is nonsense, I can't get rid of this feeling there is something more. Do you know what I mean? It's something bigger than people and birds and sacrifices and rules, something more than this life as an outsider. Maybe that baby, when he grows up, could show me that something more, that place on the inside with God.

That couple with their little Savior of the Israelites is probably getting ready to leave soon. It may be hard for them to go back to living a normal life after all of these grand and overwhelming words. I wonder where they are staying — with relatives, I suppose. I wish I could just get a glimpse of him before they leave. Maybe then I'd see that he's just a baby, and it would put all these crazy thoughts to rest. But, then there would also be the possibility I'd see something in his eyes that wouldn't let me go. I'd turn into another fanatic like Anna, only as a foreigner, people would really think I'd lost it. I don't know that it's worth the risk. What would you do? Would you look into his eyes, even if it might change your whole life? Oh, I suppose that's an absurd question. After all, he is just a baby ... isn't he?

More Than Skin Deep

Making It Preach

Our narrator shares her admiration for those who have allowed themselves to be transformed by the one true God, while remaining unsure about making that commitment herself. This telling of Naaman's holistic healing and Michal's compassionate courage and faith point to the power of God to enter the human drama and set things right. Yet, it is not because of what Michal and Naaman do that God acts. Rather, God's glory is made known in Israel so that the people of the land of Aram (Syria) will fear the Lord. But, no matter how far it reaches, how many wonders the Lord displays, humans hearts like that of this woman must accept God's sovereignty for themselves in order to be filled with the transforming joy that brings eternal healing.

Making It Play

This woman is an ancient version of what we now term a *seeker*. Tough and in control on the surface, she recognizes a spiritual yearning inside of her that she cannot satisfy. She is one of those who "tells it like it is," but unconsciously shares more than she intends about herself through relating her perspective on what has happened to those around her. Being the cook, she would certainly wear an apron over her tunic and likely have her hair hastily drawn back or covered (for convenience more than convention). She is taking a break from her duties and invites the congregation into the thoughts that preoccupy her mind and heart.

The Healing Of Naaman Penetrates Deeper
Than The Skin, And Not Only For Him

(walks in, wiping her hands on her apron, taking in the fresh air)

Some people just have it — you know, that innocence. It's like they don't quite belong to this world, and nothing in this life can snuff out the glow. That what she's like — Michal. She's scrawny as they come and must have gone through horrors when she was taken from her homeland. She was lucky to end up in my master's household, at least my master and mistress are kind. But, I've heard what happens to young girls in the hands of raiders — scum of the earth! It's no wonder she still cries out in her sleep. But, like I was saying before, in spite of all that misery, Michal has a sweetness of nature, something untouchable, but touching, at the same time. Does that make sense? What I mean is that you can't help but feel, I don't know, *cared about* when she looks at you. It's like she can see right through all my bluster and thick skin and knows I'm a fraud ... but likes me anyway. I wasn't too fond of that at first, but she tends to grow on you. Yeah, I'm gonna miss that girl.

Not that I don't want her to go home — I'm glad it turned out this way! It couldn't have happened to a nicer kid! The whole thing was set up by her God, I know that now, the God of Israel. All it took was for her to want to help her master, though that wasn't such a small thing. After all, she was just a puny kid that the mistress allowed to do her fetching. You barely knew she was there! And, after having been forced from her home and made to work for strangers, why should she risk getting whipped for speaking when she wasn't spoken to? Yet, I suppose the fact that she was so meek made my mistress less likely to take offense.

At that point, my master was desperate for some solution to the leprosy, those horrible sores on his skin that made his life miserable. And, what was worse than the pain was that the king had just released him from accompanying him on stately functions so he could seek a cure. Truth was, the king didn't want to touch him! And, who could blame him? War hero or not, Naaman's skin was disgusting. How would it look for the king of Aram to get it? Doesn't take a genius to know what the gossip-mongers would do with that information — there would be a conspiracy to knock him off the throne in no time flat, claiming the gods had blighted him or some such nonsense!

So, when Michal got up the courage to tell Naaman's wife that she knew of a prophet back in Samaria, the part of Israel that she came from, who could heal her master, she brought some hope into a despairing household. Now that, in and of itself, can be a dangerous thing, if you can't deliver. But, apparently, Michal was too naive, or too incredibly confident in her God and this prophet named Elisha, for the risk to stop her. And, when Naaman heard about it, he wasted no time in asking the king for permission to go to Israel and seek this prophet's healing. The king was just as eager to have the commander of his armies healed before word got out about his *weakness*, so he wrote the king of Israel, introduced Naaman, and basically told him to heal his general.

Well ... I guess that letter didn't go over so well. Since the king of Israel wasn't the one who could do the healing, he was a bit put out when Naaman showed up at his palace with our king's request. How do I know this? My brother, Hezion, serves Naaman and accompanied him to Israel. Anyway, the king of Israel was not in any position to heal Naaman himself, and he was not fool enough to think that if he refused, there wouldn't be war. Our king does not like to be told, "No," by anyone, and he is not known for listening to excuses. So, the king in Israel publicly tore his robes; Israelites are always so dramatic! He claimed that our king was trying to pick a quarrel with him, and the tearing-the-robes thing was his way of showing his distress and calling on his god to work out the mess before it became a full-fledged war.

And, what do you know? The God of Israel did just that, through this famous Prophet Elisha. Elisha heard about the tearing of the robes bit and sent a message to have the king direct Naaman to him so that he could heal him and prove he was truly a prophet of the one true *God*. Israelites always like to claim that their God is superior to others, sometimes even saying the other gods don't exist. Everybody else thinks they're a little *odd* that way. But, you didn't mess with that Elisha guy, either. No, sir! Naaman didn't know it, but that prophet did not like to be questioned. Hezion heard that one day, a bunch of young people came out and started laughing at Elisha and calling him "baldhead," so he called a curse down on them in the name of his God and *wham!* Two bears came out of nowhere and mauled something like forty of them! Men can be pretty sensitive about that "b" word!

But, anyway, if Naaman had known about that little incident, he might not have complained so loudly when, instead of Elisha himself coming out to meet him, he was greeted by Elisha's servant. I think Naaman was hoping to see some impressive magical spell cast that would not only heal him, but honor him as a great general deemed worthy to be healed. Instead, he got simple instructions conveyed to him by Elisha's servant. He was to go to the river — the Bordan or Jordan, I've never heard of it — and wash himself seven times, and he would be healed. Well, Naaman got indignant. Did this prophet not know the great battles Naaman had fought and won? Did he not know how much the king of Aram depended upon Naaman? Surely, he was worth more than some instructions that told him to go wash in a river, which he could have done more easily at home!

Naaman stomped away and almost threw away the only opportunity he would get to be healed. That's when my brother stepped in. Hezion may never have been strong in stature nor especially skilled with his hands, but Naaman has always valued him for his wit and understanding of human nature. So, when Hezion recognized this could be his master's only chance for recovery, he convinced the others in Naaman's service to join him in going after their master. Since it was not only in Naaman's best interest, but in their own, they agreed, though they left it up to Hezion to do the talking. And, I can tell you, words have never failed my brother! Now, I can create a favorable impression with some masterpiece I've spent at least half a day cooking, but he can do it with a simple phrase or two. When we were children, he could spin words faster than Mother could spin her wheel, and he had her wrapped around his finger tighter than any of her fine weavings!

So, it is not surprising that Hezion was able to find a way to convince Naaman to give the washings a try. He pointed out

Naaman's courage and abilities by reminding him that if the prophet had asked him to do some great feat, he would have done it. So, why not do something simple like washing in the river seven times? What could it hurt? And, yes, my brother's golden tongue once again drew the desired response. But, Hezion's abilities are clearly human skills he's cultivated — I know that as well as anyone. What happened in the river that day was nothing short of divine. Even as my master rolled his eyes each successive time he went into the water and out again, his skin was clearing up, until he had no choice but to take notice. And, one thing I admire about Naaman is that he is not afraid to admit when he is wrong or has misjudged someone.

He rushed back to the prophet, whom he now believed to be a man of God, and offered him a gift in humility and thankfulness. He was determined to see Elisha face-to-face, and sufficiently scared his servant into going and getting his master, but when Naaman saw the man of God, he dropped to one knee in respect. Hezion told me it would have actually been quite comical to see such a big and powerful man as Naaman kneeling before the small-ish, scraggly prophet, if he wasn't filled with such reverence. With the look of wonder in his eyes that young boys often have when they meet Naaman, my master offered the man of God all kinds of riches in return for healing him. But, Elisha refused, just increasing Naaman's respect for him and his God.

Needless to say, I suppose, Elisha's God, the God of Israel, is now our God. With the prophet's permission, Naaman brought earth, actual dirt from Israel, home with him, believing as most folks do that you can only worship a god on his own turf. Naaman has set up a small altar, and insists we all abandon the gods of our people to worship Naaman's God, unless we want to find another master to serve. At first, I didn't notice much of a difference; to me, one god was like the next. And, it was a relief not to have my kitchen help spending half their time preparing sacrifices, when they are supposed to be fetching things for me. Yes, I have a position of some importance. Just as Hezion is valued by our master, I am equally important to our mistress, who often has to feed commanders, while they plan strategies for upcoming battles.

Well ... even though I didn't notice a difference worshiping another god, I have noticed a difference in my master. His skin is not only restored, he has been filled with religious fervor like I've never seen before, and he seems genuinely happy. And, when the master of the household is happy, it makes life a whole lot easier for the rest of us. It has spread to my mistress, too, who often wanders into the cooking tent humming, like a young girl who imagines herself in love. But, it is not just giddy, temporary happiness in my master. It's a healing that has gone much deeper than his skin. He's even decided to send his servants to take Michal back home to Israel, not only giving up the rights of ownership, but charging them to search until they can find her family or a suitable position for her. Isn't that something? A few months ago, he almost stepped on her one day because he didn't even notice her, and now he's giving her fine garments, freedom, and a military escort! Good for her....

I just wish ... Oh, it doesn't matter. The sooner she goes home, the better chance she has of finding her family, if any of them are left. She might not like what she finds, I'm afraid — but, at least she'll be home where she belongs. There is just a part of me that wonders if, maybe ... if I would feel my master's joy if I just had a chance to talk with her before she left. I know she's busy packing, but I feel my heart yearning for something. Listen to me — I sound like a poet, or even worse — like Hezion! Still, yearning is the word. I'm yearning for something that would give me the glow I see in Michal and Naaman. It's like they know who they are, and where they are going. It's like they have seen this God and nothing in the world compares. Do you know what I mean? Ah! Maybe too many aromas in this tent have addled my brains! I am not impressed by much of anything, anymore.

I'd better get back in there and make sure those nincompoops don't burn everything I worked so hard to create! Yes, sir. The God of Israel will have to do more than heal somebody's sores to move the hearts of folks like me. *(walks away, then pauses)* But, I sort of hope it happens.

Captive To Love

Making It Preach
Distilling the essence of the gospel into truth that makes sense to the hearer is a challenge and gift. It is a challenge because a person coming back for more may depend upon that short explanation resonating with the hearer's heartfelt needs. It is also a gift in that each time we tell it, we continue to define what it means for us. Since the treasury official, unfortunately remembered as *the Ethiopian eunuch*, is credited by many with bringing the gospel to Eastern Africa, he had plenty of opportunity to tell the story. Perhaps, if those of us who are afraid to speak of our faith could remember how good the news is and that others have searched long and hard to discover its freedom and salvation, our love for Christ and compassion for others might open our lips — and our spirits.

Making It Play
There is a music and gentle rhythm in the way English is spoken by people from many African countries. Let that creep into your speech, or at least speak slowly and deliberately enough for the words to suggest it. This serving woman may not be a native of the southeastern Nile region, but it is her home. There were many queens with the title Candace (pronounced can-duh-see), and they were expected to eat much and lounge much in order to achieve an impressive girth. Thus, our storyteller is placed in an overwhelming position, sitting before this impressive leader and trying to put a newly discovered faith into words. Her body language should show nervousness as she sits and reenacts that conversation, but as God's Spirit provides her with the words, she becomes more confident and relaxed. A simple, lightweight garment without sleeves and quiet sandals or slippers would be appropriate, perhaps along with a thin bracelet or two.

The Ethiopian Official's Servant
Details His Spiritual Quest

"He's acting strange, that one. You were with him. Tell me ... tell me what happened to make my man of numbers and measures become a poet. You must know, my girl. Now, sit and tell me the story."

Those were the words that bid me, an ordinary serving girl, to sit in the presence of the great Candace of the Nile and explain something I barely understood myself. I glanced at those eyes that understood a thousand mysteries and knew not what to say. This queen, my queen, was so ... intoxicating and intimidating in her grand beauty and size, seated upon her throne of gold and ivory, her dark skin sparkling like the jewels embedded in the cup from which her lips drank. I was paralyzed, maybe even hypnotized, not only by her presence, but by the story — no, it was more than a story — by the transformation of a soul to which I was not only a witness, but was now bound. And, yet that story burned in my heart in such a way that I knew it would be no good to plead ignorance. "Yes, Your Majesty," was all I could muster.

I nervously sat upon the cushion indicated by the Candace; so stiff was I that she laughed, her voiced filled with the rich tones of the ages. "My, my, girl. Relax. I did not get to be this size by eating my people. I am not asking you to explain the mysteries of the gods. Just tell me what you saw and heard."

"But, that's just it, Your Majesty. What I saw and heard revealed a great mystery, one of heaven and earth and the consummation of their marriage. It is the joy and peace of having become part of that consummation that has filled your advisor with greater treasure than all of the wealth you have assigned to his care. I cannot presume to tell you about the mysteries, since your knowledge is that of many generations. But, if you wish, I will try to put into words what it is we experienced in Israel."

"Yes. That is what I wish." The intensity of her eyes unnerved me, and my mouth went dry. But, I knew I had to continue, not just out of duty to my queen, but out of the divine love to which even my spirit had been taken captive, gladly captive. And, thus I began, as it had begun, several moons ago.

"When you agreed to Master Menelik's trade pilgrimage, as he called it, he immediately told me to begin preparations. He told me that I would be visiting my homeland, that I would be seeing people who look like me and that I should be grateful for this opportunity. I was. Though I barely remember my parents, I did not remember anything of my homeland. But, I must say, Your Majesty, that I soon learned as we journeyed closer to Israel, that I was traveling farther and farther from my home. No more did I see the lush green of the land along the Nile and hear the calls of our beautiful flying friends. The ground was hard beneath my feet, rock was everywhere, and it was so dry. I do not know how they can survive trying to work earth that unyielding. But, it was on just such a hard, barren road that the miracle happened."

"I suppose it should not have surprised me. I should have seen how Master Menelik's heart was open, searching the heavens for answers that could not be deduced from the figures in his ledgers. Though he is usually a quiet man, not given to lengthy conversations, and though I am not of his station, not one in whom he might confide, those desert skies seemed to draw him out of himself. Because I was not strong enough to walk as many miles as the men, he occasionally invited me into his chariot. He shared the reason he was so eager to go to Jerusalem, that it was more than increasing trade between our two nations." The knowing smile and nod of the Candace prompted me to add, "I believe you were aware of his true intentions, and my master knows that he owes you a debt of gratitude for blessing his spiritual pilgrimage."

"I am sure you were able to surmise much from his name, though I was not aware of its significance until he mentioned it on our journey. 'So, you have now come home,' he began. 'But, did you know that I have, too? There is Israelite blood that runs in my veins, as well, although you might not guess by my appearance.' I must have looked startled, because he smiled and assured me, 'Ah, there is not as much of it as yours, my dear, but my parents always taught me to honor the spirit of my ancestors. Though we do not have records dating that far back, I am said to have descended from King Menelik, son of our beautiful Queen Makeda and the wisest and most prosperous king of Israel called Solomon. It is even said that one of the greatest treasures of the Jewish faith is hidden somewhere in our land. Another of my ancestors was said to have betrayed the royal house, and that is why my family is no longer considered royalty. That is also why I had to give up my masculinity to once again receive a position in the palace. It was the ultimate test of my loyalty.' " I stopped, wondering if I had said too much before a queen. I could not forget the tear that gently ran down his cheek as he spoke of it.

But, the Candace just nodded with understanding, and she offered me, a servant, one of her fresh figs, perhaps to give me time to reign in my thoughts and emotions. It was almost as if she could sense that my sadness for my master's chaste state was more than polite sympathy. As I mentioned before, my queen understands many great mysteries, the least of which would be a woman's heart.

When she motioned with glittering hands for me to continue, I did. " 'Thus,' my master told me, 'I have long been fascinated with the God of the Israelites called the Lord, and the jealousy with which the Lord always guarded them, despite the many times their leaders ignored their God's commands. It is even said that the Lord will send one to be called the Messiah, who will restore their nation to the prosperity it enjoyed under Solomon, and then proceed to bring other nations under the divine truth of this one, true God.' Well, of course I had not heard of this, since I do not have access to the news of other nations, but the idea greatly appealed to me. The desire in his eyes to mingle his different bloodlines in harmony with one universal Creator resembled my wish to blend my home, your kingdom, with my past."

"I was pondering that possibility, as I walked along the road heading away from Jerusalem. What I had seen of the temple and the priests was fascinating, but those serving the temple did not seem very receptive to strangers from another land, even one as important as my master, your honored servant. Therefore, as we began our journey back to you, I could tell Master Menelik was disappointed and frustrated because, though he had been able to purchase scrolls with the sacred writings of that people, no one had been willing to explain the many mysteries that lie within them.

And, that is why Master Menelik allowed a commoner, an unrefined teacher who was traveling along that same road, to approach his greatness without the proper manner of respect. He asked my master if he understood what he was reading, to which Master Menelik replied, 'How can I unless someone explains it to me?' A few of us could not help glancing at one another when the man told our master that he had been sent by God to do just that. But, Master Menelik did not seem startled at all and invited the man, covered with dirt from the road, to join him in his chariot. I am sure now that my master regarded this as an answer to his many prayers. And, it was."

I hesitated, choosing my words carefully, wanting to make sure my queen, the grand Candace, truly understood the importance of what she was about to hear. I silently said a prayer and felt fortunate that my queen was looking at me with interest, but also patience. "My master had been reading about this Messiah, though he did not realize it because the words from a prophet named Isaiah spoke of one who suffers and dies at the hands of his people. It was an odd mystery, indeed, to hear from this man that the Messiah would be part of God in human form, sent to suffer so that he might become king and save his people in the heavenly realms. His sorrow and death on earth were to bring joy and life for eternity to all, from any nation, who would accept his path to truth."

"And, when will this man come?" The question startled me, so urgent it was, coming from the Candace's perfectly serene, languishing form.

"That is the revelation, my Queen, the supreme knowledge that your man of numbers cannot hide. You see ... he has come." She waited in absolute stillness for more. "His name was Jesus. He was born in humble circumstances that he might know the hearts of all of his people. He taught them the truth of the one, true God and that they all belong to God and are accepted and loved no matter who or what they are. Also, he told them that God's authority and love are to be above any on earth, and that God's Spirit can fill and enhance all that is part of the pattern of life. He told them that if they believe in him and turn back to God, they will be saved for eternity. Then, Jesus was killed by men who were jealous of his power over their people's hearts and the way he led people to God through means their religion had not been able to do. But, that is not all. No, Your Highness, that was only the beginning because on the third day, just as he'd promised, God raised Jesus from the dead; many witnessed it. And, then he was first to rise to an eternal life that only he could provide. It's not the resurrection to deity reserved for royalty, my Queen, but an eternal existence in glory for people of all stations who will accept his divine gift."

I waited, not sure of what she would say or do. Finally, "I need time to ponder this revelation. I will call Menelik to me in due course, but I wanted to hear it first in the heart wisdom of a woman. You may go." As I rose, I was surprised to feel the sureness of my steps, the trembling replaced by a graceful confidence. "One more question, girl." I turned just before the archway that marked the opening of that audience chamber. "Have you accepted this gift of ... what would you call it?"

"Love, Your Majesty, and life. Yes, I have, my Queen. And, now I know who I am." I turned and walked away without once more being dismissed, but I sensed that it was all right. I knew that I, too, was all right ... as right as I could ever be.

As I pray for my queen, I will pray that you, too, might accept that gift.

Look, But Don't Touch!

Making It Preach

Lust and greed go hand in hand. They seek to gratify immediate desires, while ignoring the cost to others and one's own soul over the long term. Nainah's wisdom of years allows her to recognize the far-reaching effects of her nephew's selfish actions. The Prophet Nathan's parable of the heartless sheep owner could well be completed by these words of Jesus: *From everyone to whom much has been given, much will be required; and from the one to whom much has been entrusted, even more will be demanded* (Luke 12:48b). Nainah laments that her beloved David deserves God's wrath and warns the listener of the consequences of taking "more than the blessings you have been allotted by God." But, even from her ancient perspective she knew that God will often relent from punishing upon the sincere repentance of God's people. She alludes to the grace and forgiveness now available to us through Jesus, our Messiah.

Making It Play

Nainah personifies a Yiddish-influenced character type: the Jewish mother, or in this case, the auntie David might have had. Her pride in all of David's good qualities and accomplishments add a bittersweet humor to her disgust with what he did. Though she is elderly, and she would perhaps want to wear a shawl over the tunic and/or a long head covering fastened under the chin to make her look matronly, Nainah has a fire within her that can be expressed with quick, decisive, though age-appropriate, movements. Her self-deprecating comments about being "just a woman" are a dramatic device she uses to gain sympathy, while never doubting her own influence over David and others.

King David's Auntie Has A Few Things To Say
About His Relationship With Bathsheba

A peeping Tom ... he's the king of all Israel, and he was nothing more than a peeping Tom! Or, perhaps I should say, a peeping David! That's what started this whole thing off; he just couldn't keep his eyes to himself. And, once those eyes have wandered ... it's no use! How many times did I tell him when he was a boy, "Look, but don't touch"? And, do you think he could do it? No — I'm not sure it's in him. So, when you have a weakness like that, it is best to keep your eyes to yourself! Eh? Eh!

Who am I, you might be asking, to say such things about the king of Israel? I am his Aunt Nainah, and his favorite aunt, at that, because I do not kowtow to him like even my brother Jesse does, now, to his own son! King of Israel or no king, I've swatted his behind, and I was tempted to again over this whole affair. Adonai, forgive me! I suppose you should not take the Lord's anointed over your knee. And, what am I to say? I'm just a woman.

But, if someone were to ask me, I would tell him that what my nephew has done is shameful, destroying a family because he peeped down on that wife of Uriah while she was bathing and his thinking came from below the belt! *Oy-vey*, he was always such a good boy, except for that looking and touching thing. He feared God and was brave in defending his people. Oh, was he brave! From the time he was young, he killed bears and lions that threatened Jesse's flock, he did! Then, when no soldier would fight that gigantic Philistine Goliath, my Davichka stepped in and wiped him out with just a stone! King Saul, rest his soul, was jealous of my boy because David was more successful in battle than even the tall and powerful king himself. And, do you know, David remained loyal to his king to the end, refusing to kill him, even though Saul had tried to do David in more than once? It is no wonder the Lord picked my Davichka to be the next king. The only problem is that he was given too much, too quickly. Not that I, a mere woman, would tell the Lord how it should be done.

But, if the Lord were to ask me, I would say that when a man is given too much, he forgets to be grateful, and soon, he will not be satisfied with what he has. No, he wants more, eh? Eh! And, what happened with that woman? He touched before he thought about it and defiled himself before God. Oh, he thought if he sent her home, it wouldn't matter, no one would know, but there was one thing he hadn't counted on. She was not barren! So, mighty King, how would you explain this baby from the wife of a man who has been away from home in battle? Surely your servants and advisors would wonder.

Now, I have to give him some credit here, though not much, because he did not just set her up to get rid of her. True, it takes two to make a baby, but when you are summoned by the king, you obey. Now, I would go to my death before I would betray my husband, but she was young and perhaps *star struck*, or maybe she didn't have a choice. Anyway, David tried, twice, to get Uriah to go home and lie with her so that everyone, including Uriah, would be convinced that it was his child. However, Uriah proved to be more honorable, I hate to say it, than my nephew. He did not think it fair that he go home and enjoy time with his wife and household while his comrades were sleeping out in the fields during their military campaign. David is a sly one, he is, so he even tried to make Uriah drunk and go home to his wife. Yet, Uriah would not go. *Oy!* That poor man was so loyal, it cost him his life. And, what David did was unforgivable, making sure that Uriah was killed in battle so that he could take Bathsheba as his wife. All this because he desired that woman when he saw her! Not that I, a woman, can tell the king of Israel when he is wrong.

But, when he asked me, I told him that he should have been satisfied with his other swarm of wives and that an innocent man's blood was on his hands. He did not want to hear it, of course, but I was right, eh? The good Lord even sent the Prophet Nathan to David to tell him the same thing, using a story of a man who had many sheep, but took another man's only lamb to slaughter for guests. David was incensed by that story and declared that the first man should be punished. Only, he soon found out that he was that man! And, punishment will come; the Lord has spoken. Though David will not lose his life for this, praise be to Adonai, his household will be plagued by dissension and death the rest of David's days. Perhaps it is time I go back to my home in the hills, eh? Eh!

How one mistake can end up like this, *oy-vey!* I suppose I should not talk as if I have never made mistakes, ah, some of the things I did when I was young! Ha — there was that time with the goat! I found her wandering loose, and though I was pretty sure where she had come from, I pretended I did not and took her as my own. However, by the time I returned, the owner had been through the camp looking for her, so instead of giving her back, I tried to hide her in my tent. Have you ever tried to hide a goat? Before I awoke the next morning, she had eaten her way through my tent and was sampling my father's toes!

Ah, we all have those stories, am I right? Though, some are more serious than others. The owner of that goat got her back with just a few bruises and a stomachache. But, when we take from others, sometimes they can never get back what we took. That is especially true when it is not a thing, an object. When we take another's confidence or dignity away or do not give enough time to our families, ah, we cannot go back and change what we've done. My people put on sackcloth and ashes and fall down before the Lord and beg for mercy when we have done wrong, because there is no sin against a neighbor that is not in some way a sin against the Lord.

What is it that you do? You do not look like the sackcloth and ashes types — too shiny! Where do you go to be released of your sins? Eh? Wherever it is or to whomever you go, maybe having seen what happened to my Davichka, it would be a good time for you to stop yourself from taking any more than the blessings you have been allotted by God. Go to your Lord and ask to be forgiven of what you have taken that was not yours, and perhaps God's mercy will shine upon you and grant you peace. Perhaps you have time before your family will suffer a curse because of you. Ah, perhaps your repentance will even turn back the wrath of God and allow you to live free of curses — not that I, just a woman, would presume to tell you what you should do.

But, if you were to ask me ... Ha! *Shalom chaverim.*

What I Did For Love

Making It Preach

Sacrifice is part of discipleship. Hannah realized what too many people do not wish to acknowledge: all gifts come from God and should, therefore, be subject to God's intention for them, not ours. Samuel was a gift sought in the desperation of childlessness, but was given into the Lord's service in grateful obedience to the giver. Hannah's courage in seeking divine blessing, and in entrusting that sought-after blessing to God, is an inspiration to all who accept the gifts of God and are willing to use them in the ways and places to which they are called by Jesus. *Ask and it will be given you; search, and you will find; knock, and the door will be opened for you* (Matthew 7:7). What we do once we walk through that door is a sign of our gratitude and the measure of our faith.

Making It Play

This involves performing a dual role. The opening paragraph invites your own personal comments on motherhood or "mothering," so please insert anything you feel would be appropriate.

Adding a simple head covering may be all that is necessary to make it clear that the woman who comes back out as Hannah is not you. A light colored alb or robe would be sufficient for a tunic. Hannah has a quiet vitality, and though she is not comfortable in front of crowds, she warms up and years drop away as she shares her tale. Take time with the vulnerable parts of her story: her feelings regarding sharing a husband, being unable to conceive, and giving away her precious child. Her pain may touch similar points of pain in members of your congregation, and that will allow her words about God's healing, restoring work to have a more powerful and grace-filled effect.

Hannah Shares Her Faith, Pain,
And Praise As Mother Of Samuel

Being a responsible, loving parent involves patience, incredible amounts of energy, plus being willing and able to make difficult choices. I'm so pleased that a friend of mine has agreed to join us and share with you out of her experience, which contained one especially agonizing choice. Through her story, I hope we will learn more about what it means to trust God with the things that matter. So, I ask you to welcome our special guest Hannah. *(calls toward door)* Hannah? You may come out now. *(pauses)* Just a minute. *(go out the door, as if trying to convince her to come in, while adding the necessary costume pieces to "become" Hannah)*

(Hannah enters, hesitantly, looking a bit overwhelmed by the crowd) Uh, hello. My, there are a lot of people here! She was all bent on my talking to you, but I don't really know where to begin. Yet, because I owe the Lord my never-ending praise, I will try. *(clears throat)* Well, my name is Hannah of Ephraim. My husband is Elkanah, of the Zuphites. I have four sons and two daughters, good children, all of them important to me, but the one you have probably heard of is my son, Samuel, who judges Israel on behalf of the most high God. You may wonder why I should be so blessed as to bear such a son. I've wondered that, myself. It's actually quite a story. In fact, I think that's the story my friend wanted me to tell you. So, here goes....

You may know that my nation Israel suffers and has suffered for a long time. We could barely even be called a nation, really, compared to the powerful Philistines, who kept threatening us. Though we've known for years that we were reaping punishment for foolishly being unfaithful to our God, my people have been waiting for the time God promises us, a time of power and prosperity and peace. However, I have to admit I was never very political, nor religious, for that matter. Though our people's situation looked bleak, for me, it could never compare with the bleakness in my heart that lasted for so many years ... and the emptiness in my womb.

From the day I met Elkanah, our wedding day, I was impressed with how he treated people. I could tell from his smile and just the way he looked at me, also the servants and even the animals, that he was fair and kind. He has a great sense of humor, so he made me feel comfortable right away, like I didn't need to be afraid of leaving my family and becoming a wife. As I got to know him, he said he loved my shyness and was glad that I didn't talk his ear off all the time. He eventually came to love me, and I love him. He's really very devoted to me — except for the fact that he has another wife. Of course, having more than one wife is more common in my land and time than in yours, I've been told, but let me tell you a secret I haven't told Elkanah. I don't care how "acceptable" it is — I don't like it. Wow! I've never said that out loud before. I feel a little better, actually. Phew! Well, I guess that's not what I'm supposed to be telling you, so I better get back to my story.

As I mentioned before, I found out I couldn't have children, that something was wrong with me. And, being barren is one of the worst disgraces I could face. You see, I couldn't go out and get a job or do anything else with my life, like some of you; that just was not an acceptable option for a woman. All I had was keeping house and raising children for my husband. And, because Elkanah was so kind to me, I wanted to be able to give him offspring. Elkanah said it didn't matter to him, but it mattered to me. The more offspring a man has, the more honor he has in the community. I wanted to help him continue his proud ancestral line. I guess I also wanted to be part of it.

As if being barren wasn't bad enough, there was the little issue of that other wife that I mentioned: *Peninnah*. Peninnah thought it was just the funniest thing that I couldn't bear children, while she could. "Better get your rest, Honey," she'd say, "because you'll be doing a lot of scrubbing from now on. That's all you're good for!" I didn't see a woman when I looked at her; I saw a snake! I saw that snake from the Garden of Eden, tempting me to haul off and smack her. But, I knew that God didn't want Eve and Adam to listen to that snake, so I tried to ignore her. It still hurt, though.

I didn't want to give her nor her children the satisfaction of seeing me break down. But at night, after everyone was asleep, when Elkanah was with her, I would take a walk and look up at the stars and pray. No, not to the stars — I don't believe in praying to things. I prayed to God and figured that a God who could make all those stars could surely hear me. So, I wept, and I prayed ... and nothing changed. For years, this went on. So, I knew what I had to do. If God wasn't coming to me out in the dark, cold night, I decided to go to where God is.

When Elkanah's household went up to Shiloh to offer our yearly sacrifice before the Lord, I snuck away after mealtime. I know it was bold for a woman to go to the temple of Adonai and just throw herself down, weeping and praying, but, I was desperate! I made this vow: "O Lord Almighty, look upon the misery of your servant. Please remember me and give me a son. If you do, I will dedicate him to you. No strong drink nor razor will touch him, and he will be yours for all his days!" Later, I regretted such a rash vow, but I figured it was the only way to really get God's attention. I must have even started praying out loud, kind of hysterically, because the priest Eli approached me, and, can you believe this, he accused me of being drunk? Drunk! I have always tried to live purely, and in the midst of my despair, he treated me like a woman from the streets. Oh, if he hadn't been a man of God, and we hadn't been in the temple, I might have ... given him a piece of my mind! This was one time being kind of slow with my tongue was a good thing!

Anyway, I explained to him that I wasn't drunk, but just really upset and that I was praying with all my might. And, you know something? It worked! He believed me and said, *Go in peace; the God of Israel grant the petition you have made to him* (1 Samuel 1:17). I was amazed, and so happy, not just because of what he said, but because I somehow knew that God had really heard me this time and that I would have a child. And, I did. When I saw that little face, I knew that all of the suffering and the humiliation had been worth it. There he was, a new human being ... and so tiny. It was like I was holding a tiny miracle right in my arms. I was holding a miracle, wasn't I?

I know what some of you are thinking, though you are probably too polite to say it. What kind of a mother would give her son away? You think I wanted to? I'll admit that until I gave birth, it was all about producing a male child to make Elkanah proud, to vindicate me, and even, God forgive me, to make Peninnah eat her words! But, once I looked into his tiny eyes, I didn't think I could ever let him be away from me. Then, I remembered the promise I had made to God. Though I knew he would be in the best of hands, doing the most honorable job he could do, leaving Samuel in Shiloh with the very priest who'd thought I was drunk was the hardest thing I have ever done. But, I've learned that when you give that pain to God — I didn't know what else to do with it — God will eventually give you other joys in other places. It never gets rid of that loss, of that barren place inside you, but other blessings rain down and bring up new grass and flowers. For me, it was in other children that God allowed Elkanah and I to share, as well as later learning that our Samuel would give guidance to our people. We need someone like him speaking on our behalf before God.

Do you have anything you promised God, but haven't given up, yet? It doesn't matter if you're a man or a woman or who you are, really. God doesn't forget those things you promised, and even though you might have had second thoughts about sacrificing something for God, I can tell you that God will fill the space it leaves with other blessings — the best blessings there are. God keeps promises, too. You should know that! I was told you've even met a great king sent by God to save you! What a day that must have been! Knowing him means that it's not too late for you to do something to get things right with God. You see, the rewards are not only comforting for you now, they keep coming for eternity.

Well, I've said everything I can think of. Those were more words than I've spoken all together in a very long time! I'll leave you to whatever it is you were doing. Thanks for listening to my story. Maybe, someday, you'll tell a story of your own.

Year C

Epiphany 2
John 2:1-11

Pass The Wine

Making It Preach

Mary's musings foreshadow that great day when all believers will feast together with Christ in the kingdom of heaven. It is a feast to which people of all stations and situations will be invited, as Jesus alluded to in Matthew 22 and Luke 14, though not all will accept the invitation. Mary celebrates the unity forged through the lifeblood of her son, our Savior. Though she presents her story in the spirit of feasting while the bridegroom is still with us (Matthew 9:15), her references to wine are bittersweet reminders to us that Jesus gave of his own blood, the wine with which we commune, to bring eternal life to our party. Therefore, hers is the invitation extended each time we partake of Holy Communion: drink deeply of Christ's gifts of salvation, heed his *nudges*, and step with faith into God's unfolding plans.

Making It Play

Once a mother, always a mother! Mary can't quite keep her pride hidden after her son's first display of heavenly power. The strength and faith that have allowed Mary to survive and thrive, despite wagging tongues, arduous travel, and the death of her husband, are evident in the way she seeks to advise (or *nudge*) this very special son. A simple, yet festive head covering, along with a tunic and sandals would help the congregation to step back into a first-century wedding feast. A chalice for the wine should be used or pantomimed in the final toast. You may wish to invite a couple of children to briefly join you in the roles of Mary's grandchildren, though you could easily indicate their presence with gestures. Remember, she may be a grandmother, but Mary is probably only in her mid- to late-forties at this point. No need for a cane and white wig!

Mary's Pride And Prejudice
Regarding The Wedding At Cana

Doesn't she look radiant? He's a bit rough around the edges, but I get the impression he is pleased with the match, too. I can sense these things. Oh, it's such a frightening and exciting time for them ... I remember at my wedding, though, I was carrying an extra "burden" she does not have. But, that burden turned out so handsome — look at him!

I'm sorry; I never introduced myself. I am Mary of Nazareth, and that is my oldest son, Jesus, with those fishermen who follow him everywhere. Thankfully, the smell of their trade is starting to wear off! *(looks around)* I'm not sure where my other children have scattered, but these are my two oldest grandchildren, Joseph, named after my dear husband, may he rest in peace, and Naomi. *(licks her thumb and proceeds to wipe something off the little girl's face — then sends her off)* They grow so quickly!

What do you think of this celebration? It's one of the nicest I've seen — especially the wine! Excellent quality, am I right? You want to know a secret? I realize this was only meant to convince those fishermen friends of his, but sooner or later everyone will know who he is — my son, I mean, Jesus. You may well think that I am either one of those sickeningly proud mothers or that I've enjoyed a little too much of this fine wine, but I hope that our God will help you to see the truth. A miracle happened among us. Few understood it as such, but it was a miracle, nonetheless!

In the midst of the celebration, no one noticed there was a problem, but if it hadn't been remedied it could have resulted in dishonor for our hosts and a lot of grumpy people! They thought they had enough wine, and it really is hard to judge how much people will drink, but it happened — a host's worst nightmare! Yes, the wine ran out! It was only the third day of the feasting, and the only reason I knew is because I happened to walk by when Eli, the groom's father, was talking with the master of the banquet. I could see the look of panic on Eli's face, and ... well, I know it was rather forward of me, but I've always been a romantic, and I hated to see the festivities ruined. So, I quickly stepped forward before Eli had a chance to tell him there wasn't anymore, and I said, rather, blurted out, "But, Eli, I'll get my son to bring out the rest of the wine. You just go and enjoy yourself." It's amazing how much one look can say, and his was no exception, but he cautiously left us. With an air of confidence I didn't really feel, I asked the banquet master which of the servants could assist my son.

Now, my son, on the other hand, is not quite as easily manipulated. Actually, manipulated isn't the word I want. I shall just say I have a talent for encouraging people to do what is in their own best interests, as well as the common good. Though my son has always resisted my attempts to utilize this particular talent with him, he cares very much about the common good, and that is the reason I prevailed in this case. However, it took some whisperings from the Lord to give my unspoken suggestion credibility. After all, mothers don't know very much!

"Jesus, they have no more wine." His fishermen friends expressed their disappointment with the prospect of ending their festivities, but Jesus' sour look was directed at his mother before it was quickly hidden behind that mask of indifference he wears whenever things don't go his way.

"Dear woman," he said, as if I were some poor, demented creature, "why do you involve me? My time has not yet come." His favorite fisherman, the big one with the loud voice, looked at us with surprising intelligence in his eyes, but didn't say anything.

I gave Jesus one of those looks that Joseph used to tell me could stop a Roman legion, and I walked over to the servants that had been summoned and simply said, "Do whatever he tells you." I then walked back to the party, having faith that my stubborn, yet steadfast, son would do the right thing. What thing is that? Oh, I'm sorry. Whenever I talk about Jesus I get carried away and forget that not everyone knows how very special he really is. This is where you may have trouble believing me, especially since we just met, but I ask that you at least give me a chance to explain.

When I was just a young girl, betrothed to Joseph, but not yet married, I had a visit from an angel of the Lord. I know what you're thinking, that it was a dream or an emotional fantasy of a romantic girl, but I swear to you that later events confirmed it was an angel. His name was Gabriel, in fact. Anyway, I won't test your patience with too many details that are hard enough for me to believe, but suffice it to say that I was told my child, not yet conceived, would be great and would save this nation! I understand that he looks like countless other men who are here to enjoy themselves — ah, now he's dancing! But, I knew that God would give him special powers when the time came.

Well, strangely enough, when I heard that the wine had run out, I knew it was time. Already thirty years old, Jesus has gotten used to waiting, but I felt God's Spirit nudging me to nudge him! Have you ever felt that nudge inside of you to tell someone something important or to do something a little risky? Good, then you know what I mean. And, I'm guessing you also know how important it is to pay attention to those nudges. I rather like that word — "nudge." Maybe that is a good description of that God-given gift of mine I mentioned earlier ... the ability to, tactfully of course, nudge, for one's own good and everyone else's!

Anyway, Jesus felt the nudge from me, but more importantly, from God, and he told the servants to fill six stone water jars, the large ones used for ceremonial washing. I told you before that I walked away prior to this, but I'm not so lacking in curiosity that I moved out of earshot! The servants filled the jars, though I noticed a raised eyebrow. And, there were a couple more when Jesus then instructed them to draw a glass and take it over to the master of banquet. But, all pretense of hiding their surprise was dropped when they noticed that what they held no longer looked like water. In fact, it looked suspiciously like wine!

The banquet master's astonishment did not flow from the same source, since he thought that Jesus and the servants had simply done what I'd said by supplying the extra wine. His astonishment appeared when he tasted the wine. Yes, as you might have noticed, this wine is of far better quality than the first. And, as he pointed out to the bridegroom, most people share their finest wine at the beginning, rather than saving it until the guests' taste buds are too impaired to appreciate it!

I understand that it must seem a rather bold statement to say that my son turned large containers of water into huge quantities of valuable wine. And, even if you were willing to go that far with me, you might think this a frivolous use of divine power — am I right? But, you see, it is all part of something much bigger, a great series of events known only to God and leading to places and people I can only guess.

This I know, however, that Jesus will somehow redeem the people of Israel and take his place on David's throne, to rule forever. That is what the Angel Gabriel told me: yes, I am saying that he is the Messiah! I held that back before because I feared you would not let me finish what I have to say to you, but now I pray that at least some of you will know the truth of God. You have no reason to believe me. You have no proof of the miracle I mentioned beyond the unusually high quality of the wine you now consume. But, soon, if you have ears to hear and eyes to see, the power of Jesus will become known throughout our land, and, someday, throughout the world! Not all will believe in him. Some will even try to harm him and others because of him; I know that as surely as I breathe. It was foretold by the old prophet, Simeon, when we brought Jesus to the temple for circumcision. He said that my heart would be pierced as with a sword because of him.

But, now, we celebrate! And, soon, you will know of what I speak. Some of you will recognize his beauty for yourselves: a generous heart and spirit, a wisdom that is as unsettling as it is enlightening, an iron faith and knowledge of God that will not be compromised and cannot be outsmarted, out-argued, not even out-nudged ... believe me, I've tried! For now, the wine flows freely. Someday it may not, and you may find yourselves drinking a memory. But, it will be a memory of life, the life somehow created by Jesus, according to God's hidden plans.

So, pass the wine. Drink from it freely. Savor its flavor, and know that it is given as a gift, not only to the bride and groom, but to all who drink of it. It is the wedding feast that brings us together, and perhaps by remembering this wine we share, and learning of the one who created it, we may feast together again, someday, in a time of peace and freedom and joy. *(toasts)* To life! Let it be so!

I Will Never Forgive Her — Never!

Making It Preach

Forgiveness is not a natural human impulse. That is why extraordinary examples, such as Joseph forgiving the brothers who sold him into slavery, point directly to God's intervention. That type of witness made by an uncle or someone else we know makes Jesus' sacrifice and offer of a forgiven life take on flesh and possibility for us. The disappointments and changes in the life of Reuben's daughter have begun to work the maturity in her that is sought in Hebrews 5:14, as evidenced in her graceful acceptance of the many changes in her life. Yet, she also demonstrates how with each new offense to our sense of self, we can be pushed back into a vindictive defense mode. Continual preaching and reflection on forgiveness and the Holy Spirit's power to help us with this are so important for that reason.

Making It Play

The fury born of keen embarrassment bubbles out of Reuben's daughter as she bursts onto the scene. Due to her mention of remarriage and the years Joseph spent in Egypt, she is definitely well into her adult years. However, when annoyed by family, she does the typical return to acting like a wronged teenager. Her tunic and head covering would be made of less heavy (due to the climate), yet more ornate material (due to Joseph's status), than other Middle Eastern garb. Her appreciation of what God has done in the life of her father and uncle, she readily admits. But, when reminded of her sister-in-law's wounding words, she is not ready to follow their example. It is not until the last moment of this monologue that she realizes she needs to follow suit. She needs to make that realization obvious to everyone present before she walks off.

Reuben's Daughter Learns How Difficult It Is
To Forgive Like Uncle Joseph

(Runs out, obviously distressed; not pleased to see people in front of her) Oh, what are you doing here? *(about to walk away, but stops)* Hey — I'm sorry. I didn't mean to take it out on you. You didn't mean any harm, unlike my own family! Word has spread that I am ungrateful to be here in Goshen, to be in the lushest part of Egypt, while all of the surrounding country is suffering a horrible famine. My own parents just walked past me shaking their heads, with such disappointment in their eyes. And, why? Because if a mountain were set upon my sister-in-law's tongue, she'd just keep wagging it until it crumbled away! Now, letting a few surprises out of the bag is one thing, but she has gone too far this time. Way too far! My loyalty is now being questioned by the entire family. And, why? Because when I shared with her the simple yearning of my heart to see my homeland again, not necessarily live there, she could not keep it a secret between us. She "accidentally" mentioned it, of all times, while serving drink at a meeting about all the herds amongst my father's brothers and their sons. If it was not for the fact that I am related to them, I would probably already be sold into slavery, like Uncle Joseph! And, it is only a matter of time before he finds out, now the most powerful man in Egypt outside of the Pharaoh. I will never forgive her — never!

I really don't mind it here. We are treated with special respect, due to Uncle Joseph, although we are not allowed to call him that if there are any Egyptians around. We have to bow down low and call ourselves his servants and other things like that. It's all a big show, since Uncle Joseph is one of the most down-to-earth people I know. Not that he was always that way! He's only five years older than I am because my father Reuben, Uncle Joseph's eldest brother, is quite a bit older than Joseph. So, I remember well how arrogant my uncle used to be. I just punched him when he got too full of himself and told me about his grand dreams, although I could never stay mad at him. But, my father used to come home shaking his head when Joseph told his brothers about dreams in which all his brothers, who were sheaves of wheat or stars or something in the dreams, bowed down to him. My father loved Joseph, but even he got awfully tired of him. And, he was worried that some of my other uncles were ready to string him up someplace and leave him. Yet, when he tried to have a talk with Uncle Joseph, it didn't do any good. Uncle Joseph just laughed, rolled his eyes, and changed the subject. And I, for one, would have followed him anywhere. He was too much fun for me to stay irritated with him! At least, that's what I thought. That's not, however, how my other uncles saw it.

The wool finally fell away from the sheep when Grandpa Jacob bought a beautiful coat for Uncle Joseph from the traders passing through. It had long sleeves and looked grand, far nicer than anything we could have come up with there. But, he did not buy anything so nice for his other sons, which was typical, since Grandpa had special love for Uncle Joseph. Uncle Joseph is the son of Grandpa's beloved wife, Rachel. My Grandma Leah, may she rest in peace, though she was the most wonderful person you could ever know, was taken care of by Grandpa, but not really loved. It had to do with some mix-up about who Grandpa was supposed to marry ... I don't know the details. We are not supposed to talk about it. So, Joseph was favored because of his mother. Although, he also had the power to charm Grandpa like he did me, so maybe his mother really didn't matter that much. Whatever the reason, it just fed his ego and made his brothers resent him that much more.

So, that is when it happened. My father and his brothers had been grazing the flocks down at Dothan, and Grandpa sent Uncle Joseph to see how they were faring. When the brothers came home, they brought his fancy coat, torn and soiled with blood, saying Joseph had been killed by a wild animal. Of course, Grandfather did not take it well, and neither did I, for that matter. But, I was surprised at how hard Father took it. I knew he loved Joseph, but I had never seen him look so beaten. And, when the rest of us had grieved and were picking up the pieces of life, Father did not come out of it. Mama and I were worried about him, and others learned to steer clear of him because he barely spoke to anyone, and that was in a low growl. He eventually became less irritable, but from the time of Uncle Joseph's death, he was a different person; he always looked as if he carried the weight of the world on his shoulders. The kind, gentle, and tolerant father of my childhood was no more, and I missed him. I gave up hope that I would ever know him in that way again.

But, our Lord God, who has a special relationship with Grandpa Jacob, is good and merciful. I should not have given up hope. Many years later, when Grandfather sent his sons, except young Benjamin, who is Rachel's other son, down to Egypt to buy food, who did they find? I guess Uncle Joseph played with them a bit at first, but who could blame him? Yet, when all was said and done, Uncle Joseph let them know who he was and actually forgave them! He had obviously grown up a lot since we were kids! Just as a wine's flavor becomes richer and more mellow over time, Uncle Joseph's struggles had been the wineskins needed to turn him into an honorable servant of the God most high. You see, he not only forgave his brothers, he invited all of us to come down here and live in some of the best land that Egypt has to offer.

And, Father is finally himself again! He smiles at the children, tenderly holds my mother, even in front of others, and he leads the songs and prayers of praise we lift up to our God. I just couldn't believe it, and I mentioned it to Uncle Joseph. That is when it all made sense. Uncle Joseph told me that Father sought him out, after he had invited the family to come live here. Father fell at his feet in tears and begged his forgiveness. Apparently, my father had suggested the brothers throw Uncle Joseph in the cistern instead of killing him, planning to sneak back later to rescue him. However, when he returned from checking on the flocks, he found they had sold Uncle Joseph into slavery. Father could not forgive himself for not standing up to his brothers, since he was, after all, the eldest. He knew he should have stopped their plans before they got going — and he should have. So, the guilt of not doing enough plagued him all those years that Uncle Joseph was in slavery in Egypt. Of course, Father did not know how Uncle Joseph's crazy ability to dream was a gift from God, and that Uncle Joseph would eventually interpret one of Pharaoh's dreams. The advice he gave to Pharaoh about what he saw in the dream, about the years of good harvest followed by famine, landed him the best job in Egypt!

Anyway, my father lives again, so to speak, because he knows he is forgiven. Do you know anyone like that? It is amazing to see, really! And, since Uncle Joseph became God's special servant, it means that the great God Almighty must have forgiven Father and his brothers, too. Father obviously felt horrible about what he'd done, but there was really no way to make up for it. Finally, he was forgiven, anyway. As Uncle Joseph says, our Lord God had a plan that was accomplished through this mess, and if God has a plan, who are we to stand in its way with bitterness and grudges?

So, I suppose that was a rather long way of explaining how I came to be in this place, so far from my homeland. The hill country where we lived was also beautiful and not so hot, but now the grass there is withered and barely anything will grow. We have been truly blessed to be here in a place that still has food to spare, thanks to Uncle Joseph, and, of course, the Lord God! That is why the comment I made about wanting to see my home was just a touch of homesickness. Who can blame me for that? There have been a lot of changes in my life lately, with the famine, losing my husband, may he rest in peace, an uncle back from the dead, and, then, making a sudden move. Who wouldn't reminisce about the days that were stable? It is certainly not the kind of thing that should have me "on the outs" with my family. I even agreed last week when Father said he had made a marriage arrangement with one of the men of this land, a righteous man, according to Uncle Joseph. Remarriage was certainly nothing we could contemplate in the midst of the famine, after my husband died; may he rest in peace. But, agreeing to marry here means I know I would never go back. Oh, I suppose my parents think that word of my supposed discontent will sour the marriage offer. You see? My life could be ruined, all because of one woman's words — as if she didn't have enough other words to keep her occupied! Why is this happening to me?

Well, one thing is becoming clear. I had better go tell Uncle Joseph myself, before he hears the twisted version that came out of her mouth. I am trying to start a new life, which is not an easy thing to do, mind you, and she has to go and throw a shepherd's crook into it! I will just explain to Uncle Joseph that I meant no harm, that I was just homesick, and maybe he will talk with Father and my intended. He still remembers the days I put up with him dragging me around in a headlock! That should count for something, right? And, maybe he will find a way to punish that sister-in-law of mine, so that she can't do any more damage! He's the most powerful man in Egypt, isn't he? He can certainly teach her a lesson! No, sir, don't expect to smear his niece's name in the mud and get away with it. That's practically the same thing as betraying him, and you know he'd never stand for that! No, sir, no mercy, especially when the cruelty comes from someone who is supposed to be part of the family. *(said while walking off in triumph until the truth hits her — she stops)* Oh! *(lightly smacks her forehead and walks off)*

Here We Go Again

Making It Preach

Compassion fatigue is a very real threat to committed Christians. Jesus regularly went away by himself to pray, and after a particularly long day of spiritually and physically feeding a multitude, Jesus sent his disciples off in a boat to give them a break while he dismissed the crowd (Matthew 14:22). However, the disciples in Joppa did not necessarily understand this pattern of sabbath renewal as an important part of staying fit for ministry. Our churches often do not, either, and we end up losing some of our most valuable lay and clergy ministers to burnout. Tabitha's testimony underscores how Jesus can turn our life experiences into gifts for those who are hurting. But, it also reminds us to deepen our connection with Christ and spread around the work of ministry for the sake of God's glory, the empowerment of Christ's people, and the transformation of heavy burdens into joyous opportunities.

Making It Play

Tabitha has a strength of character refined in life's fires. The congregation meets her at a crossroads between where she would like to be and where she finds herself. The Apostle Paul articulated it this way: *For to me, living is Christ and dying is gain* (Philippians 1:21). With a wry smile, as Tabitha lays out her story, she sets about convincing herself that being thrust back into her earthly ministry is best. She could be in the process of bringing more garments to the widows, giving her hands something to do as she tells her story. Despite the wealth in her family, she likely dresses simply in solidarity with those to whom she ministers: a tunic, head covering, and sandals.

A Resurrected Tabitha
Reflects On Life And Ministry

There they are. Here I am. It is so much the same, yet absolutely different. I had not realized how important this ministry is to the other disciples ... and to God. Sure, the widows appreciate it. To them, these hastily sewn garments are precious because they are new and clean and — free! They have no means with which to buy the material to make their own, even if they could. If they did, some of them would have sewn circles around me in their day! They've told me as much. In fact, a few whose eyesight is still keen and whose fingers are not too gnarled have offered their services, and that is the reason the quality of the tunics and cloaks has improved! Praise God for their talent! But, I provide the material, and I do feel a calling to care for these women, to comfort them in their losses and illnesses, so I guess I belong here, as well. That is why I'm back. My name is Tabitha.

Oh, no, I didn't go anywhere ... well, actually I did, but it wasn't the type of trip one takes every day. I went to be with my Lord, *the* Lord, Jesus the Christ. Wait! Before you politely make excuses so that you don't have to listen to lunatic ravings, please know that I'm as sane as any of you. It's just that I was the recipient of a miracle. I was dead! The Apostle Peter — good, you've heard of him — he prayed, and God thrust me back into this life. One moment I was floating in the warmth and peace of paradise, and the next thing I knew, a man's voice commanded me to get up! I was a little shaky at first, as you might imagine, but he offered me his hand, and there I was, in an upper room where we often meet for meals and prayer and discussion of Jesus and the Hebrew Scriptures. Then, he escorted me down the stairs as if I was a princess. I still had no idea who he was, but seeing the joy and tears on the faces of not only the widows, but the disciples, brought a lump to my throat. I knew I had to hide my true feelings, so I put on my best smile, greeted everyone warmly, and thought, "Here we go again!"

That sounds ungrateful, doesn't it? I don't mean to be. I prayed fervently after it all happened for Jesus to forgive my selfishness. You see ... I didn't want to come back. Please don't misunderstand me; I had found working with the widows and poor families rewarding, if also exhausting. Those children are bundles of energy, even when they haven't been eating properly, and they have so much love to give! But, I did it all in anticipation of the day I would see Jesus return, so that more hearts would be ready for him. When I became ill so quickly — something inside of me stopped working, I accepted my fate because I knew I would be in the heavenly realms with Jesus, and then return with the other believers when he transformed this earth to the kingdom of God. Never, in all my wildest dreams, had I imagined I'd return before him! So, though it doesn't excuse my reaction, I hope it at least explains my hesitation at jumping back in.

As I said before, though everything and everybody looks just the same, it is not. I am not! You cannot return from a dance with the divine and not be a little starry-eyed. I'm a bit bolder, for one thing! Having grown up in the shadow of such a powerful earthly father made me feel rather small. He began a merchant fleet with just one small boat that he'd put all his money into, and he spent his first season patching it after every voyage! But, he was savvy and personable and able to convince others to invest in his business venture, and in twenty years he was running one of the most successful shipping enterprises on the Mediterranean, headquartered here in Joppa. I was always in awe of my father, who had little time for me, though he took an interest in my brothers once they were old enough to learn the principles of sailing and shipping and business. I was married off to the son of one of his most lucrative trading partners, a manufacturer of dyes. I did not even think to object, though my intended was Greek and had been drunk each time I met him.

Gregorius did lay off the drink long enough to enjoy his new plaything, that's what I was to him, but he could not lay off indefinitely. He spent less and less time at work, less time at home, outside of sleeping, and his reputation was rather infamous. His father had to buy him out of more than a few embarrassing situations. Gregorius was so out of control that his mother and other women stopped looking at me askance for not producing children, and simply looked at me with pity. I can't say that was much of an improvement. I was too timid to confront him about his problem and my loneliness, so I spent a lot of time in prayer. Though his family had a shrine and they prayed to their household goddess, I was allowed to pray on my own to the Jewish God, the one true God. I could not go to synagogue because my husband would not convert to my religion, but I quietly observed the rituals of my faith that did not interfere with the social interactions in this Greek family. Kosher meals were definitely out of the question!

And, it was my faith that consoled me when the drinking finally made Gregorius ill, and I decided to nurse him. His mother did not think that was appropriate, since we had many servants, but she also did not know what else to do with me, so she said very little. It was during this time that my husband and I finally became friends and shared some tender moments, but it was too late. His skin turned a horrible grayish-yellowish color, and he wasted away.

It was while I was walking to clear my head of the grief and uncertainty about my future that I saw a crowd gathered around the doorway of a small synagogue. They were listening to a traveling teacher. I pulled my head covering down farther so that no one would recognize me, and I moved in, wanting to hear what this strange man had to say. "Who is he?" I heard someone ask behind me.

"Says his name is Philip. Says he has news of the Messiah!"

Well, that caught my attention! I moved as close as I could to the doorway to try and make out what this Philip was saying. When I heard the name Jesus of Nazareth, I started looking for a quick way out of the crowd. Whenever that heretic's name was mentioned, riots followed! I saw the look of displeasure on the face of the rabbi, but could find no graceful way out. "Wonderful!" I thought! "My husband has just died, and I will be found trampled to death in a place I am not even supposed to be! The rabbis will probably say it is my punishment for marrying a drunken heathen!"

But, God's face smiled upon me, upon us all, because Philip's easy-going manner and careful use of phrases like *I believe such and such* or *I'd like you to just pray about and consider these things* made him seem less of a threat. Well, I did pray about his words, about this Jesus, and found myself seeking out the places Philip would go each day to teach us more about Jesus. One day we met by a small pool of water trapped near the sea, since the rocks made the shore too dangerous, and I was baptized along with several others. I knew then that Jesus would be the "man of my life."

However, there was the issue of my future. My oldest brother, Dominic, had taken over the business after my father passed away, just over a year before Gregorius died. Since I had no children, there was no reason to stay with his family, so I went back home to help with my mother, nieces, and nephew. Though my brother hinted at my remarrying, he saw that I was increasingly getting involved with good works to keep busy, so he did not push. My family was politely tolerant of my belief that the Messiah had come and offered forgiveness of sins; they knew I was still grieving the loss of my husband. As time wore on, though, my sisters-in-law and mother began to believe and were even baptized secretly. But, since followers of the way of Christ were not popular, they knew my brothers would not approve of their open participation, fearing it would hurt the business. So, my mother and sisters-in-law would help when they could from home, but I was the only one who was known to be a believer in Jesus. I became the family "eccentric," but I didn't mind because it made it easier for me to come and go as I pleased.

Since I was a widow myself and realized that my family's wealth and good will were the only reasons I had means of support, I felt a special calling to help other widows who were not thus blessed. And, as I got to know these women and their neighbors, helping to distribute food to the poor and nurse the sick, I discovered that new, clean clothing was an expense poor women and families could not afford. Though I had never had to sew, I had learned to do some needle work to pass the time during my lonely marriage. Therefore, I decided to put that knowledge, if not an actual skill, to work, and I began to make garments. The recipients of the first tunics were very gracious, considering the bloodstains from pricked fingers, so I knew the need must be great. Soon, other women believers started to help, and I found myself organizing that and many of the efforts on behalf of the poor. But, I did

113

keep sewing because I found it more enjoyable the better I became — fewer needle sticks, anyway. I would report back to the disciples, and they seemed pleased with our efforts. However, when they started to invite me to the discussions in which decisions were made regarding our community of believers, I felt a bit overwhelmed. I wasn't used to men asking for my opinion, and when they began to refer to me as one the disciples, I felt a great deal of pressure. I would not give up my service to the Lord Jesus, but I found that I was more and more anxious and tired as the days, weeks, and months wore on.

At first, when the illness struck, I thought it was just that I could not keep up with everyone's expectations. So, I'll admit it: It was a relief to die and hear those glorious words of Jesus spoken to me, "Well done, good and faithful servant. Enter into the joy of your master!" I did not realize that the words of that parable that resonated through my spirit, saying I had been faithful in a few things and would be put in charge of many things, meant sending me back! I thought they were preparing me for joyful service in God's kingdom, not the ghetto of Joppa!

"I will be there, soon!" I hear the women laughing and calling to me, and in their voices I hear the voice of Jesus lingering ... encouraging. It is not easy to be a follower of the way of the Christ. Yet, I know something others don't know. I've seen something you've not seen. I believe with certainty. Like Mary of Magdalene, I can say that I have seen the Lord! There is no place for insecurity, no need for fear anymore! Take your place with him, serve him, and you'll see. Someday, you'll see it all! "I'm coming!" May it be so for you! *(exits)*

You Want Me To Do What?

Making It Preach

Tolerance of differences, forgiveness of others' weaknesses, reserving judgment are all noble concepts that are easy to live by in theory. But, when confronted with them in our own lives, self-protective instincts often get in the way. Philemon's wife, possibly Apphia of the superscription, and her husband are being faced with putting their newfound faith into practice on a personal level. They are being asked to do something out of sheer obedience to Christ and love for Paul that seems unwise. Yet, it was Paul who said, *No, God chose what is foolish in the world to shame the wise ...* (1 Corinthians 1:27a). Apphia, used to privilege and getting what she wants, weighs the cost of discipleship. In so doing, she challenges the congregation to discover the ways they too are being called by God to make the changes and choices necessary to be obedient followers of Christ.

Making It Play

Apphia, a relatively wealthy Greek woman in Colossae, is dressed to suggest that she is a woman of means: quality garments — a stola with a pala draped over it, expensive-looking jewelry, and possibly some hair adornment. Agitation has her pacing as if she is presenting her case before a sympathetic jury. Her voice would be cultured, her posture confident. Emotion tries to squeak through when she speaks of Paul introducing her and her husband to Jesus, but is quickly hidden by her self-control. She should be less guarded when she finally figures out that this is about more than Onesimus. Here, the congregation becomes partner with her on the difficult journey of actually living out the faith they claim.

Philemon's Wife Explains
Why Paul's Request Is No Small Matter

(shakes her head) Onesimus? Onesimus! Of all the people God has brought into our acquaintance, wouldn't you know it would be Onesimus who gains favor with our holy brother, Paul? Onesimus ... his name means "useful," even "beneficial" in our language, but let me assure you, that young man has been everything but! Okay, he does have a winning smile and pleasant enough disposition, but that slave has got laziness down to an art form! The work he does accomplish is not through his own labor, no, it is generally at the hands of one of the maids whom he has wrapped around his finger. We even caught my daughter running an errand for him! I think that is what finally set Philemon off!

My husband is actually a very generous man, and for years he would just shake his head when he found out about one more of Onesimus' antics. Neither of us could help but admire the lengths to which that young man would go in order to avoid breaking a sweat. However, with each caper he managed to pull, Onesimus became increasingly arrogant, and arrogance is something Philemon has little patience with — especially since his conversion.

Actually, it was I who first heard of Paul of Tarsus from my cousin, Philia. She invited us to her home for a meal one evening with friends and was very excited about this *outrageous upstart* — her terminology — who would be there. He had explained to her household that the Messiah of the Jewish faith, a Jesus of Nazareth, had been crucified by the Roman authorities and had risen from the dead so that all people, Jewish or otherwise, would be forgiven their sins and brought into a relationship with the God of the Jews. Neither I nor my husband could fathom why anyone would want to be in a relationship with the God of the Jews, since they never seem to have any fun, but we thought we would humor my cousin and meet the odd fellow. Certainly, he must have some interesting stories to tell of his travels, and we could always excuse ourselves early to check on our children if he got too long-winded. Little did we know that it would be those long-winded speeches that would change our lives ... save our lives. I get choked up when I think of ... well, that's a story for another day. Back to Onesimus and our concern at hand.

You see, about six or seven months ago, Philemon was feeling ill, and he told Onesimus to bring an important message to the manager of one of our orchards. However, apparently something, presumably female, caught Onesimus' attention on the way, and the message was never delivered. Well, this resulted in a huge shipment of fruit being shipped to a destination that refused to accept it, and before it could be returned, it rotted. So, the manager sent a letter of distress to my husband, not even knowing that he was ill, which was delivered back into Onesimus' hands at our estate. But, Onesimus, not being able to read and noticing it was a beautiful day, decided to take a break and lounge by the pool. Finally, when my nine-year-old, Dorcas, ran by, he gave the message to her to give to her father. I have never heard a sound quite like what came out of my husband's mouth that day. I was on the other side of the compound and decided it might be a wise decision to stay where I was for the time being. Well, of course my husband gave Onesimus a thorough "chewing out," though he didn't have him whipped, as many people would have done. Then, he assigned Onesimus to do some real labor in one of the orchards for a couple of months. Onesimus was stunned, and indignant we later found out, so he decided to steal enough money to get him far away, and that was the last we'd heard of him ... until yesterday.

We received a letter from our dear brother, Paul, during the heat of the day and were relieved to hear that his spirit is not broken, despite his prison sentence, which seems interminable. Though the letter was primarily addressing Philemon, Paul's desire to keep us accountable to one another and to living by the way of Jesus comes through loud and clear. True to form, he made the letter an epistle, to be read aloud to the entire congregation of believers who meet in our household. It's rather difficult to ignore it that way. And, yes it's true, Paul has somehow connected up with the charming, infuriating Onesimus, and feels great affection for him — he even says that he has been as a "father" to this impetuous slave! We love Paul truly, but how our Lord and Savior Jesus of Nazareth could pick such a gullible man to found our church is beyond me! I know Onesimus ... he has probably presented a convincing testimony of conversion to Paul and has wormed his way into the man's heart, but I am afraid that it is nothing more than a clever act — and a convenient one at that, considering that Paul is the one man, other than Jesus himself, to whom Philemon feels indebted.

Oh, I'd like to believe that Onesimus has found faith in the forgiving grace of God made available to all people — which, I know, includes criminals and slaves — but following the way of Jesus is costly and takes passion. It takes a willingness to work hard and risk your neck for your belief and for others. That doesn't quite match the description that pops into my mind when I hear the name *Onesimus.* Paul is asking Philemon, voluntarily, to set Onesimus free so that he may assist Paul in his ministry. Of all people! Philemon would be far more appropriate to take up such an honorable assignment, or any number of others here in Colossae, even other slaves! Philemon, who by law could severely punish or even execute Onesimus if he were that sort, is being asked to find it in his heart to forgive the boy and welcome him, as if he were welcoming Paul. You know, the neighbors already think we're walking the fence by letting people of the lower classes come to our home to worship — if we set a slave free, especially a criminal, when he has not even so much as purchased his freedom ... that would be the last of the invitations to the theatre and some of the best feasts in town!

But, then again, Jesus of Nazareth was also considered to be a criminal. I feel as if we will be hanging on that tree with him if we trust someone so untrustworthy, if we forgive one who has betrayed us! You are asking us to do what, Paul? Play the fool before our entire household, our fellow citizens, our congregation of believers? *(pauses)* Yes, that's exactly what you're asking us to do. It's not really about whether or not Onesimus is sincere and deserves forgiveness, is it? Which of us deserves forgiveness, really? This isn't even about Onesimus! It's about us, and whether or not we will let the Holy Spirit change us ... here ... inside. This all reminds me of that passage of scripture proclaimed by the Jewish prophet, Jeremiah. God told him to go and observe a potter at work.

The potter was shaping a vessel, but then destroyed it and reworked it into another vessel as he saw fit. Perhaps, we are being reworked by our Creator from the inside by way of the one person we might most resist.

Oh, don't look so innocent. You may not be asked to set a slave free ... that would be perfectly acceptable in your day and age. But don't be mistaken; God is still working on your hearts, shaping and molding you to fit into your place in the kingdom of God. What does that mean for your life? How are you being asked to change from the inside out? What are you being asked to risk? We're not so very different, you and I. We are all forgiven and loved by a God who does not ask how much we owe, nor how trustworthy we've proven to be in the past. And, that same God lays before us a blank page upon which the next chapter has yet to be written. Do you have your pen ready? Be careful what you write. It just may come back to haunt you ... or save you.

Proper 19 / Pentecost 17 / Ordinary Time 24
Luke 15:1-10

Lost And Found

Making It Preach

The woman searching for a coin is in need of what Christ and his church have to give: the assurance of God's love and forgiveness, a focus beyond herself, economic assistance, and an accepting community. Yet, she channels all of that anxiety into the frantic search for a coin. The first woman's lack of enthusiasm at actually finding the coin represents the disillusionment so many humans experience when worldly goals do not ultimately satisfy. Yet, like the woman at the well, she discovers that only *living water* can keep her from thirsting again and again (John 4:5-42).

The shepherd's wife functions as an angel, in the Greek definition of *messenger*, if not a heavenly being, and offers a portal of grace through which the other woman could walk to find what she truly seeks. She embodies the joy Jesus tells us the divine Shepherd feels when the lost coin and lost lamb return safely into divine arms.

Making It Play

Though the staging of this is more difficult, the one actress will have a blast with these *two* women! The woman searching for the coin is probably neurotic, if not obsessive-compulsive, and needs to find far more than a coin! The shepherd's wife should sound as if she has just arrived from *jolly old England* and is both frightening and endearing in her energetic love for the Shepherd and lost sheep before her. Both characters spoof modern concepts, but do so in an ancient context. Therefore, they should look like they could have been Jesus' neighbors, complete with a simple broom and shepherd's staff.

When both women speak, they should face the congregation. The woman's house turns; not your general direction. Remember, there is a natural suspension of disbelief with any dramatic piece. The first woman addresses the congregation as if they have come to purchase a chicken. The second addresses the first woman as if she is in the congregation, though you can make her spot a reference point to which your gaze returns at crucial moments. We rarely look into someone's eyes continuously, and in between those looks your gaze can include the congregation. The switch from character to character can occur by simply making a 360-degree turn, setting down the broom the first time and picking up the staff in the process.

Searching For A Lost Coin
And Lost Sheep Yields Brand New Discoveries

(frantically sweeping the floor — talking to herself) Oh dear ... oh dear! How am I ever going to find it? So many cracks and hollows in the floor. It could have rolled into a corner. It could have — Uhhhh! I don't even want to think about where it would be if it rolled outside! *(getting hysterical)* I — I — I think I'm getting a migraine. Slow down ... shallow breaths ... soothe the inner child. *(closes eyes and calms down)*

(opens eyes and sees congregation) Oh — hello. Nice to see you. *(uncomfortable silence)* Why are you here? Oh, yes, the chickens. Of course, the chickens. The chickens are — outside. You do see them, don't you? They are rather hard to miss. So, why don't you go — and — pick out a chicken — out there. Very good.

(under her breath) Some people's children! Anyway, back to my search. *(resumes sweeping)* It must be here someplace. I just can't imagine that it went beyond this room. I had them at the table, counting all ten drachmas. I know! I'll retrace my steps, that's what I'll do, I'll retrace my steps! Let's see, I took the jar from this shelf and then I walked to the table where I dumped it out and — Ahhh! *(starts, seeing congregation again)*

You know you really shouldn't keep sneaking up on people like that. I seem jumpy? Well, you'd be jumpy, too, if someone

122

kept creeping about behind you! Well, I see you've chosen your hen. Good! I hope you enjoy her — she's a good egg producer, that one. Have a nice day. Oh — yes, payment, of course, payment. *(holds out hand for coin)* Thank you. I'll make sure I hold onto this one — unlike — oh, what? Something wrong? Why would you think there's anything wrong? Anyone could forget to ask for payment ... or lose a coin ... *(breaks down)* even a whole drachma!

Go ahead! You can leave me. It's not your problem! Even though the income left by my husband is dwindling, and I can hardly live on what the flock produces, it really isn't anything you should trouble yourself with. What? You don't mind helping? Oh, bless you. Praise be to the God of Abraham, Isaac, and Jacob, not to mention Sarah, Rebekah, Leah, and Rachel! I just can't seem to find it on my own, and my sister won't help me out. She and her family live over there, but she doesn't like to be around me when I get nervous. And, I do seem to be nervous a lot, but I am not obsessive-compulsive, no sir, that was a low blow! My therapist doesn't think so, either.

Anyway, when I last saw the coin, it was on this table. Don't ask where it came from. I am a widow and an easy target for some smooth talker to cheat out of her only means of survival! Not that you look like smooth talkers, but it is better to be safe than sorry. Anyway, the coin was here *(points)*, and now it's gone! I've swept this portion of the floor, but if you wouldn't mind starting over there, we can meet somewhere in the middle. *(hands over an imaginary broom)* Thank you, so much! Thank you, Adonai. You won't forget your people!

(turns around, puts her own broom down, and picks up shepherd's crook) My, busy as bees, you are. It's going to be a very clean house, though! I'm sorry to barge in like this, what with all this sweeping fervor, but have you happened to see a lone shepherd without a staff? My Jerry forgot it again when he ran off to find his troublesome little lamb. Cute as a button, she is, but always wandering off into the thicket here, into a cave over there, down into crevice so tight my young son was the only one small enough to get in with her. Then, we had to get both of them out! Now, that was a merry scrape, it was!

Wait a minute! You're looking for something, too, I can just tell it! I suppose I can share with you now that all that sweeping of a clean house looked a bit obsessive-compulsive to me — not that I'm one to judge. You know who you remind me of? The woman that Jesus chap spoke of, who lost a coin, lighted a lamp, swept the house, and searched and searched until she found it. Dearie, you'd better sit down. You don't look so good. Posies and promises, that is you, isn't it? And, I see you've enlisted help — good idea! Don't worry, Jesus said you'll find it, and believe me — he knows!

That's not all he said, either. Stop and take note of the joy you feel when you find that coin, and you'll get an idea of what God feels like when one lost person repents of his or her sin and returns to God. Lost could mean any number of things, I suppose, not just forgetting where your staff is when you rush off to find an errant little lamb! My Jerry has such a good heart, and such a bad memory! I can tell you that I'm sure God appoints angels to watch over all of the little lambs, and big ewes and rams, too!

Why, did you know that you have never left God's sight, not for a second? If you have been lost, it is only because you haven't looked closely enough to see the outline of your Shepherd, who always watches over and cares for you. And, the exciting part is that no matter where you've wandered, even if you've fallen into a hole and cannot seem to get unstuck, he calls to you. And, when you hear his voice, you'll know your Shepherd. And, when he reaches out his staff, like this, you can hang onto the end, then he will pull you out and save you. And, not just from that hole, but from whatever pit of sin and despair you've toppled into!

So, don't you see? The Good Shepherd's staff is always before you, unlike my husband's. It is simply your choice as to whether or not you wish to grab on. *(holds staff out to them)* Grab on! No? Oh well, I'm not the one you need to be hanging onto, anyway. I get so excited when I think of all the openings in the Lord's flock! Dear me, I've taken up too much of your time. *(sets down staff and leaves it)* If you've not seen Jeremiah, I'd better seek him in other pastures. Ha — a little joke there. Other pastures! Well, happy hunting. Oh, by the way, Jesus also said that when you find the coin you will be so happy that you will rejoice with your neighbors. A little party would be just the thing, don't you think? Don't forget about us; we're just over that hill. Well, so nice to have had this chat. Toodle-loo! *(steps away, turns around, sets down staff, and picks up broom)*

(mouth open, weakly waves, bewildered) Do you know her? *(shakes her head to snap out of stupor)* Anyway, we're sure to find the coin if we stick to my plan. Yes, sir, my plan is always the best, well ... almost always. I suppose it doesn't seem as if I planned very well this time, does it? But, I did, we did, I did after my husband died, and so far that has set me in good stead. Well, it has almost always set me in good stead, except in times like this, when I realize that I can't find something, a coin that my husband's hired hand would have earned for a full day's work! That was when we could afford to have help, but I had to let him go, of course. So, I'm here — here I am, just me and the chickens, the chickens and I, and I really do get — lonely.

Ugh! Wasn't that woman annoying, what with all her cheerfulness and talk of shepherds and bonny little sheep? I don't understand how someone can be that — happy! What with one of the lambs always wandering off and a forgetful husband, I don't think she has a right to be that confoundedly joyful!

I wish I knew her secret. I haven't smiled like that since my daughter's wedding. Praise be to God that was back when we were able to give her a nice dowry. But, now she's gone to another village, and my sister doesn't really like me very much, and her children look at me as if I've got leprosy and I — I — I think I'm getting a migraine, again. Slow down — shallow breaths — soothe the inner child. Oh, who am I kidding? That inner child is me, all of me, and all of me not only needs soothing, I need healing. I'm broken. I need to be pulled out of the river, or the hole, or whatever blasted analogy she used! See any shepherd's crooks to hang onto? *(spots the staff that was left)*

What's this? I was only joking, you know. How remarkable. She must have left this behind. Quite a pair they make, if they are both this careless! Ha! I knew it was too good to be true. Unless ... no. We've already wasted enough time. Are you going to help me look, or what? What? You think she left it on purpose, don't you?

Now, why would she do that? She never gave me a chance to get a word out of my mouth, how could she possibly know what I was thinking and feeling? Of course, she did say that there are angels watching over all the lost lambs. What was that she said about needing to see the shepherd? Now, I wish I'd paid more attention to her ramblings! Oh, well, she's probably just as crazy as she sounds. *(picks up coin)*

Oh — here it is. Here it is! Praise be to God, I found it! We found it! Thank you so much for helping me look. It was right near my feet the whole time! I'm thrilled — really — I'm ecstatic — I guess. For some reason, I don't feel that joyful impulse to have a party. Could I make you some tea, or something? No? Well, I sure am glad that's over, at any rate. Too much stress is not good for a person! Thanks again. Me? Oh, I suppose I'll feed the chickens and check for eggs. The house is certainly clean enough! Then, who knows? Maybe my crazy neighbor will have found her husband, and I can bring his staff back. Yep, I think I'll do that. I've got a question or two for her, anyway. May the Lord bless and keep you under the watchful eyes of the Shepherd! *Shalom.*

Pour Water On My Head, But I Won't Go Away!

Making It Preach

With this parable, Jesus lifted up to his disciples their need *to pray always and not lose heart* (Luke 18:1). That type of persistence is much easier spoken of than practiced. Due to lack of faith in God's power to answer prayer, feelings of inadequacy in our praying, fear of what prayer answered might mean, and plenty of other reasons, we tend to pray only for short periods of time on a *need-to-pray basis.* Persistent prayer takes hard work, and it is easy to get discouraged when we do not see obvious results. But, the trust this widow sings of is what it is all about, trust in God's love and God's desire to give us good things. That is especially true since Paul assures us that the Holy Spirit takes our prayers and makes them acceptable to God. We do not have to look to the Bible to see examples of answered prayer; they are all around us. As it is written in the epistle of James: *The prayer of the righteous is powerful and effective* (James 5:16b).

Making It Play

If a neighbor were to wake up and witness this confrontation, one comment might well be, "That is one tough old lady!" The circumstances she faces give her the opportunity to put her take-charge philosophy into practice. Though older, energy seeps from her pores, and she probably finds as much satisfaction in the battle as she does in the victory. Her appearance should be subdued and conservative, perhaps even diminutive beneath her tunic, head covering, and shawl. This will create a memorable contrast when she

127

starts heaving rocks onto the judge's roof. Have her go ahead and say the "boom-boom-boom" sounds. That is a part of her dramatization of the story.

The Persistent Widow Shares Her Recipe For Success
(enters, singing the spiritual)

> *I will trust in the Lord,*
> *I will trust in the Lord,*
> *I will trust in the Lord*
> *'til I die ...*

You wanna know why?

Ah, of course you do. I can tell, you're sitting on the edge of your seats! You're in the house of the Lord, and you want to know you're in the right place. Well, you are! And, I'll tell you why I am so sure that you are. You got a few minutes? Of course you do — that's why you're here.

You've all got prayers you need answered, right? Prayers for healing, prayers for forgiveness, prayers that you'll be able to resist your favorite little temptation so you won't feel embarrassed to come before God: whatever they are, you've all got prayers you need answered, right? Of course you do, that's why you're here. So, how often do you pray those prayers? Once? Twice? Twice a week, or maybe three strikes and you're out, God? No, that's not what Jesus told you. He told you to pray always and not lose heart! That's what he said, he sure did, right before he started talking about me — yes, me! Didn't know I made it into the big book, did you? Yeah, big name, bright lights! I even made it into the title of the section that nice person just read: The Parable of the Persistent Widow. That's me!

And, why do you suppose Jesus would start talking about me right after he told his disciples to pray always and not lose heart? It's because I don't give up! There are people who have some unpleasant words for that quality, but I prefer to say that I am diligent or persistent, like the title says; if somebody knocks me down

128

in the mud, I get right back up again, and they hear about it, too! My mother always said I cause too much trouble, that I have to learn to give and take, that I have to accept the things that don't go my way. Ah, bushel baskets! I always believed that you'll never get anywhere unless you go up to the gate and ask to be let out! And, what do you know? Jesus must not think that's such a bad way to be, since he dreamt me up!

Now, I had to be tough, okay, because when my husband died, I didn't have legal rights to anything! I wouldn't have minded if Jesus would have waited to dream me up until women had a few more rights, but it's his parable, not mine. Anyway, since we had no children to inherit the land, my husband's brother was dead, and the next of kin didn't care about the land, I kept the farm running. I had to hire a foreman to take my husband's place, but it looked as if the farm would continue to turn a profit, and I would be secure.

I should have known better! I told you I was persistent; I didn't say I was cunning. One day my neighbor sent his workers to till two-thirds of our land, and claimed it had been his all along. I couldn't pay a foreman and survive myself with the profit from only one-third of the land! My husband's uncle, the next rightful claimant of the land was too old to fight, so I had no choice but to step in! I went to the judge charged with handling land disputes. I brought the papers proving my husband's ownership of the entire property. And, you know what he told me? "I'm sorry, ma'am. I can't help you. Perhaps you could go live with your husband's uncle. Perhaps he will have pity on you." Pity? Pity! The last thing I wanted was pity — if my mother had heard that, she would have warned him that he had really done it and had better prepare for battle. And, though I don't believe in violence, that is exactly what he was about to get!

I found out where he lived; don't ask me how — I have my sources! I waited until the dinner hour when I was sure he was sitting down with his family to a big meal, and I knocked on the door. Well, he was a bit irritated that I interrupted his meal, but his wife had already let me in, so he would have appeared heartless to throw me out at that point. He told me I could wait in the next room. Well, I waited and waited, while the family finished up and went their separate ways, and when I finally heard footsteps coming toward me, it was his wife with a plate of food. "So sorry you lost your husband, dear. I hope this will help." That was all she said, and walked out. She thought I was there for charity, and I was too stunned and frustrated to catch her in time to explain. That's what that heartless, godless man told her, so she believed him. Well, I fed that plate to the oxen on my way home, realizing that I would have to be more direct on my next visit.

And, there was another visit, all right, that night, when the moon had passed over halfway through the sky. I approached the house quietly, barely a peep from the chickens, and armed with my biggest soup ladle, I banged on the door so hard that the hinges creaked! When he finally shouted, "Who is it?" I shouted back just as loudly, "I want my land back!" When he told me to go home, I just kept banging until the entire household was awake. He opened the door and looked as if he wanted to wring my neck, but due to his family standing there, he said with tight lips, "Come to the city gate tomorrow, and we'll see what we can do." Well, I wasn't prepared to receive another hearing so soon, so I went home, rejoicing in my victory. But, remember I said I was persistent, not cunning? He never showed up! I waited all day, but the other elders said they had not seen him, either. Though tired from my excursion the night before, I decided it was time to pay this nice family man another midnight visit.

This time I brought stones, carefully concealed in my apron in case soldiers saw me on the road at night and suspected me of making trouble. So, when I got to the judge's house, I started throwing stones up on the roof so that they would make all kinds of racket when they landed. And, just in case he didn't get the hint, I shouted praises to the Lord, and appropriate acclamations about our Lord, from Psalm 146:9, that would give his whole family no question as to the reason I had come. *(heaving stones up on the roof)* "Praise the Lord!" — boom-boom-boom. "The Lord's name be praised!" — boom-boom-boom. *"The Lord watches over the strangers; he upholds the orphan and the widow"* — boom-boom-boom — *"but the way of the wicked he brings to ruin."* BOOM —

that was a big one! Well, what do you know? I saw the whole family at the window, mouths open, not sure what to make of me. "I want my land back," I simply told them.

Well, it looked as though I had moved them; one of the younger sons even came running out of the house toward me. But, instead of stopping before me, he headed over to the water trough, and the next thing I knew, I was soaking wet. That little urchin! But, I refused to lose my dignity. The wife was clearly embarrassed about her son's actions, and as she came out to scold him and apologize, I told his father, "You can pour water on my head, but I won't go away until you give me back my land." He looked at me, rolled his eyes, then he saw his wife giving him the kind of stare that only a wife or mother could get away with. Finally, in a voice of pure exhaustion, he told me he would go to my neighbor the following day with reinforcements and make sure that my husband's land be returned to me until a kinsman redeems it. I challenged him, still in the hearing of his family, "How do I know you'll show up this time?" "He will be there," his wife said carefully, therefore ... I knew he would be.

So, "What's this got to do with prayer?" you may ask me. You have a couple more minutes? Of course you do, that's why you're here! You see, as Jesus pointed out to his disciples when he laid out my story, "Will not God grant justice to his chosen ones who cry to him day and night? Will God delay long in helping them?" Ah, bushel baskets! Of course not! If somebody as evil as that judge will grant justice after a couple of sleepless nights, God will surely grant it simply out of love. Now, I do have to caution you. That justice may not always look the way we want it to up front, but we have to trust that God knows what it's supposed to look like better than we do! I didn't exactly count on getting soaked to the skin by a boy no taller than my hip! But, it worked out! And, if you think hard enough, I bet every one of you can think of many prayers that have been answered, or even wishes satisfied that you didn't even think of as prayers. So, just because it sometimes seems like things aren't going your way, is that any reason to stop praying and stop trusting in the Lord? Of course not! You know that. That's why you're here!

Now, join me in these words, first sung by people who went through an awful lot that was not an answer to prayer, yet continued to pray without ceasing.

I will trust in the Lord,
I will trust in the Lord ...

Amen.